FamilyCircle®
2000 Hints & Tips

FamilyCircle®
2000 Hints & Tips

Great Ideas for Managing Your Time, Your Home, Your Self

From the editors of
FamilyCircle®

MAIN STREET BOOKS

DOUBLEDAY

New York ● London ● Toronto ● Sydney ● Auckland

B / T   640.41   12.95

3/2000

A MAIN STREET BOOK
PUBLISHED BY DOUBLEDAY

A division of Random House, Inc.
1540 Broadway, New York, New York 10036

MAIN STREET BOOKS, DOUBLEDAY, and the
portrayal of a building with a tree are trademarks
of Doubleday, a division of
Random House, Inc.

Library of Congress Cataloging-in-Publication Data
Family circle 2000 hints & tips.
   p.cm
   1SBN 0-385-49445-9
   1. Home economics. I. Title: Family circle 2000 hints and tips. II. Title: 2000 hints & tips.

TX158 .F27 2000
640'.41—dc21   99-057203

A Roundtable Press Book

For Roundtable Press, Inc.:
Directors: Marsha Melnick, Julie Merberg,
   Susan E. Meyer
Senior Editor: Carol Spier
Book Design: Kathleen Lewandowski
Illustrations: Laura Cornell
Copy Editor: Virginia Croft
Layout: Smythtype
Editorial Assitant: Carrie Glidden
Production: Bill Rose

For Family Circle Magazine:
Editor-in-Chief: Susan Kelliher Ungaro
Creative Director: Diane Lamphron
Executive Editor: Barbara Winkler
Managing Editor, Lifestyle Publications:
   Joanne Morici

For G+J Publishing:
Books & Licensing Manager: Tammy Palazzo
Books & Licensing Coordinator: Sabeena Lalwani

Cover illustrations by Laura Cornell

If it is to be, it is up to me.

The simple but strong message of these 10 two-letter words is a personal favorite of mine. And since you've picked up this book, I know that you, too, are a doer and a dreamer. That's why the editors of *Family Circle* published this lively and fact-packed guide filled with our best tips and tricks. We believe this book will help make your life easier, better organized, and more enjoyable.

Since I've been an editor at *Family Circle* for more than 20 years, I've personally benefited from hundreds of our magazine's most helpful hints and shortcuts.

I thought I'd share my five favorites with you.

1. Lost the back of a pierced earring? Break off a pencil eraser and use it as a temporary fix-it.

2. Can't find your car in a parking lot? (And you don't want to set off the alarm with your remote key.) Keep an old but identifiable hat perched on the shelf behind the back seat.

3. Ring marks on furniture? A little dab of toothpaste (not gel) works wonders.

4. Melted candle wax in pretty votives? Put glass holders in the freezer for a few hours; the wax will shrink and pop out easily.

5. Can't stand mosquitoes outdoors? Plug in a fan outdoors. Its gentle breezes will refresh you on a hot day while keeping these pesky critters away.

Tips and tricks can make all our days run smoother. But the best advice of all is to make time for fun and play. Remember: "Your life is like a coin. You can spend it any way you wish, but you can only spend it once!"

Susan Ungaro, EDITOR IN CHIEF

CONTENTS

INTRODUCTION

We pack a lot of living into our daily lives. Home, career, school, kids, volunteer work, social events—you name it and most of us are probably doing it. Every minute is precious, so anything that makes our lives a little easier, frees up some time, eliminates a step or two, or solves a problem quickly is a godsend. Although we're inundated with ways to obtain all kinds of useful and helpful information—CD-ROMs, videos, the Internet—we're more likely to turn to someone we trust—a friend, co-worker, neighbor—for the solution to a problem. Why? Because if it worked for them, it'll probably work for us.

However, you can't always rely on that person to be there when life's little emergencies crop up—spilled red wine on an heirloom tablecloth, or a crayon "masterpiece" on your freshly painted wall. That's why FAMILY CIRCLE 2000 HINTS & TIPS is so valuable. An encyclopedia of useful information, FAMILY CIRCLE 2000 HINTS & TIPS is that reliable friend, filled with sound advice, practical hints, and road-tested tips for easier everyday living. Organized in a way that relates directly to what's important to you—*Your Time, Your Home, Your Self*— FAMILY CIRCLE 2000 HINTS & TIPS puts simple solutions at your fingertips. You're sure to find the right answers for everything from fixing a clogged drain to organizing shoes in a closet. It's a book you'll turn to again and again. And, like a trusted friend, this reference guide is always there with the help you need when you need it.

Joanne Morici, EDITOR

●SECTION 1●

YOUR TIME

"Nothing makes time more valuable than knowing exactly what to do with it."

T. S. Eliot

Cures for the "Where Is It?" Blues

You don't need to be a super sleuth to find what you're looking for . . . all you need is a plan.

You probably spend at least an hour every day looking—or helping someone else look—for something critical that's been "misplaced." The hints and tips in this chapter will help you put the things you need where you need them most, returning "lost" time back to you.

Color Your World

Choose a color for each member of your family so you'll know at a glance what belongs to whom. Use this for:

● Sheets: When a bed needs changing, it's easy to pick the right sheets from the linen closet.

● Towels: When you spot an errant towel left on the bathroom floor, you'll know in an instant who left it there.

● Hangers: When you take clean clothes out of the dryer, put them directly on a color-coded hanger. It's a breeze to figure out what goes where—just look at the hangers.

● Laundry baskets: By assigning a different color laundry basket to each member of your household, clean laundry can be sorted, folded, and put in the appropriate basket. When it's time to put laundry away, everyone knows which basket is theirs.

● Underwear, socks: Use indelible markers in your family "colors" to identify similar-looking socks and underwear. A small dot on the toe of matching socks and on the waistband of underwear makes it easy to see whom it belongs to.

● Keys: If you've got several drivers in your house, use different color key rings and key jackets to help you keep track of the various sets.

Know What You Have

● Storage closets and boxes are great—if you know what's in them and can find what you want easily when you want it. To help you keep track, create a "master inventory file." As you're packing away things in a storage box, make a list of everything you've got in that box and then label the list and box identically. When you stow the box—in the attic, garage, or basement—note where you've stored it on your list. Then put the list in a binder or folder that's been subdivided by storage rooms or content categories. When you want to know where something is, you don't have to unpack. A quick scan of your inventory list will indicate in minutes where what you're looking for is.

Create a rainbow coalition to simplify your life.

Kitchen Cabinet Policy

If your pantry closet resembles a food museum, it's time to take stock of what you've got and keep track of what you have. Here's how:

● Alphabetize your spices—from allspice, celery seed, and cinnamon right on through to thyme and turmeric. You'll be able to retrieve the desired spice in the time it takes to say A, B, C—and you'll be able to spot a missing spice quickly.

● Store envelopes of gravies, sauce mixes, and soups in an empty child's shoebox on a shelf in your pantry closet. Envelopes stay upright, are easy to read, and don't get buried in the bottom of your closet.

● Group like ingredients together. Bake often? Then keep the baking powder, baking soda, flour, sugar, and brown sugar all together on the shelf. If Mexican food happens to be a frequent house specialty, you may want to gather your most-used ingredients—chili powder, cumin, taco shells, hot sauce—in one place.

● Keep a shelf-by-shelf list of what's in a cabinet tacked to the inside of the cabinet door.

● Or paint the inside of your kitchen cabinets with blackboard paint. Then use chalk to list the items you need to replace. This list will help you compile your weekly grocery shopping list.

Cleanser Caddies

● A carpenter's apron—available from almost any hardware or home improvement store—holds everything you need to clean the house: an old toothbrush, a sponge, dust rags, furniture and window cleaners. Because you carry all your "tools" with you as you move around the house, you won't waste time searching for supplies. When you're done, stow the apron, restocked with any necessary fresh supplies, in one place. Everything's ready to go to work when you are.

● Another handy—and free—way to keep cleaning supplies together is to store them in a cardboard six-pack container. The cans and bottles you need will stand upright in the separate compartments. The handle makes it easy for you to tote supplies from room to room.

● A time-consuming—as well as annoying—household chore is picking up and putting away all the little things you find scattered about—loose change, game pieces, pet toys. But if you wear a fanny pack while you clean, you can just tuck those bits and pieces in the pack while you continue your routine. Empty the pack at the end of the job so you avoid running back and forth to put things away.

Catchall

● Another "catchy" idea for little odds and ends: Keep a bin or basket in the family room to hold game pieces gone astray. That way everyone knows to look there first when a checker or other game piece is missing from a set.

● When you get a new puzzle, use a colored marker to "dot" the back of each piece. Use a different color marker for each new puzzle. When puzzle pieces from different puzzles get jumbled together, it's a snap to sort the pieces.

Library Books

If you have children each checking out several library books a week, it can be a hassle rounding up all their books for return. Here are a few ways to keep those loaners from getting lost:

● Allow children under 10 years of age to check out as many books as they are old; that way you'll know how many books need to be returned.

● Keep a laundry basket or other large open receptacle in the room where your children are most likely to do their reading. Deposit library books in the basket as soon as you come home from the library and make everyone do the same after reading a book. That way you won't have to launch an all-over-the-house hunt for the books at the end of the week when they need to be returned.

Rack 'em up! A spice rack keeps beauty clutter to a minimum.

It's Not Easy Being Green

● Garden tools can be easy to lose once they're placed on the ground because the handles (often wood) and heads (usually dark green or black) blend in with the terrain. To make them more visible, paint the handles a bright color—yellow or orange, for example. Bright fluorescent-colored electrician's tape wrapped around the handle is another eye-catching option. An added safety bonus: The greater visibility makes it less likely that someone will accidentally step on or trip over a tool left lying on the ground.

Bathroom Breakthroughs

● Keep the medicine cabinet free of grooming-gear clutter. Attach a large magnet to the inside of your medicine cabinet to secure tweezers, manicure and hair-trimming scissors, and nail files.

● Mount a spice rack on the wall beside your dressing table to hold lipsticks, nail polishes, and other small beauty items.

● Screw a cup hook on the side of your mirror for hanging your blow dryer or curling iron.

● Keep tub toys tidy in a mesh lingerie bag suspended from a faucet.

The Efficient Kitchen

● If you have a pile of lids for plastic containers and pots spilling out of a kitchen closet, try this: Store a dish drainer in the cabinet near the stove, then use it to "file" lids by sizes. It's neat and you won't waste your time trying to pair up container and lid every time you need one. Also, color-code lids to containers with indelible markers so you know which two match up.

● Are your kitchen drawers filled to the brim with utensils and gadgets? Here's one way to clean up the clutter: Install a tension-type curtain rod inside or underneath a cabinet near your stove. Hang "S"-type hooks from the rod, and then hang your utensils. The utensils are within arm's reach and easy to spot. Best of all, you've got more room in your kitchen drawer.

● You'll never have to look for measuring cups and spoons if you leave them right in the sugar, coffee, and flour canisters.

● Certain household chemicals should never be mixed—ammonia and chlorine, for example. To ensure you don't mix them, attach a sponge to each cleanser bottle with a rubber band. Not only will these dedicated sponges keep chemicals apart, but you'll always have a sponge at the ready when you need it.

● It's the same thing every year— you're ready to light the birthday candles but the matches are nowhere to be found! Once again, a rubber band does the trick—just use it to affix a book of matches to the candle box.

Check, Please

● To make it easier to pay your bills, tuck stamps, return address labels, and pen into your checkbook register. You're ready to write checks anywhere.

Not-So-Remote Control

● Attach one half of a hook-and-loop fastener strip to the back of the TV remote control, the other half to some place near where you're likely to be sitting or lying down when you're using it: the underside of a coffee or end table, the headboard of your bed. When you're not channel surfing, attach the remote control to the sticky strip so that you'll always know where to find it.

Linens and Things

● Can't find the pillowcases to go with those sheets? Here's an easy way to keep linen sets together: Fold the sheets neatly to fit inside the matching pillowcase. The set is complete when you're ready to remake the bed.

Take-Along Crafts

● An old lunch box, toolbox, or fishing tackle box makes an excellent container for kids' crafts items— scissors, ruler, glue, crayons, paper. There's plenty of room, it locks tight when it's closed, and it's easy to pack up and take along to keep your child happily occupied on long car trips.

● Keep a fanny pack filled with pipe cleaners and beads, and wear it when marketing so that your kids will have something to do while waiting in line.

Where Did I Put That?

Once you've found a place for everything, how do you keep track of what you put where? Use this chart as the master list.

	GARAGE	ATTIC	BASEMENT	SHED	OTHER
Household Items					
Carpenter tools					
Costumes					
Extension cords					
Extra house and/or car key					
Fire extinguisher					
Garden tools					
Holiday decorations					
Lawn furniture					
Power tools					
Snow shovels/ice pick					
Wrapping paper/ribbons					
Miscellaneous					
Sports Equipment					
Baseball stuff					
Beach balls/beach equipment					
Bowling balls					
Camping gear					
Fishing pole/tackle box					
Skates					
Skiing gear					
Sleds					
Tennis stuff					
Seasonal Gear					
Bathing suits					
Beach towels					
Boots/galoshes					
Coats/raincoats					
Hats/gloves/scarves					
Personal Items					
Bank books					
Extra checks/checkbook					
House deed or rental lease					
Insurance policies					
Mortgage/loan agreements					
Photographs/photo albums					
Safe deposit key					
School records/military papers					
Tax forms and information					
Will					
Yearbooks					

Ready to Go

● If you're involved in several committees, here's one way to keep your sanity: Pack all the materials you need for each committee in a canvas tote bag and store it in the closet where you keep your coat and purse. When you've got a meeting to attend, grab your coat, purse, and canvas bag, and you're off.

Best Bets for Baubles and Bows

● Store pairs of earrings, small bracelets, and necklaces in the separate compartments of a plastic ice cube tray. The tray fits nicely inside a dresser drawer and keeps delicate chains, beads, or earring wires from becoming tangled. Styrofoam egg cartons also make great jewelry trays— and they're free!

● To display costume jewelry, use your kids' old stuffed teddy bears and soft dolls. These keep your jewelry box from getting cluttered and give new life to toys your child no longer plays with.

● Clip hair ribbons to a wide fabric belt hung from its buckle on a nail in the closet door. Bows stay fresh and crisp and are easy to match up to an outfit. This works for pairs of barrettes too.

Plush toys provide a pretty—and playful—way to organize costume jewelry.

Tooling Around

● Use Peg-Board in the garage, basement, or workshop to keep tools organized and visible. When every tool is hung on the Peg-Board, outline each one with an indelible marker. This way you'll know where each tool goes when it's removed from the board. You'll also be able to spot a missing tool quickly.

● You can recycle old plastic 35mm film canisters to help keep small drill bits from getting lost. With an awl or pointed screwdriver, poke a few holes in the lid of the 35mm film canister. Insert the drill bits through the holes into the canister so they stick out slightly. Store canisters on a shelf in the workroom.

● Old baby food jars make terrific containers for screws, bolts, nuts, small nails, and tacks. To keep your workbench neat, screw the lids of the baby food jars to the underside of a shelf above your workbench. Now screw the filled jar to the lid. Because the jars are made of clear glass, you can see what you need at a glance.

Wrap Artist

● Keep everything you need for wrapping packages in a tall plastic kitchen garbage pail. Store rolls of wrapping paper upright, then fill the can with other wrap necessities: tape, ribbon, tissue paper, gift cards. When you're done, stow the pail in a closet until next time.

Great Gadgets for Keeping It All Together

Sometimes all it takes is a few well-chosen accessories to help restore order to a room.

BASKETS

In all kinds of shapes, styles, and sizes, baskets can be utilized in every room in the house.

Bathroom Buy small plastic baskets to fit inside vanity drawers. Put like items, such as nail polish, files, cotton balls, and nail polish remover, together in one basket. Group medicines and other health aids—thermometers and bandages, for example—for children in another basket that's stored in an upper cabinet. This comes in especially handy when illness strikes in the middle of the night; you won't have to grope around for everything you need. Employ larger, shallow baskets to store extra bathroom necessities—toilet paper, soaps, shampoo—under the sink. Use another one to hold bathroom cleaning supplies.

A tisket, a tasket—group your household stuff in a basket.

Bedroom Small baskets inside dresser drawers keep things sorted. Use one for socks, another for panty hose. Larger, decorative baskets are ideal to store seasonal bedding, heavy blankets, and comforters for winter; lighter blankets and throws for summer. Hint: Put a dryer fabric-softener sheet in the basket with the blankets to keep them smelling fresh.

Kitchen Tiered hanging baskets come in a variety of colors to coordinate with any kitchen. But don't think of them just as storage for fruits and vegetables. Hang one near the dining table, then use it to keep napkins, silverware, and place mats handy.

Den or study Suspended over a desk or workstation, tiered hanging baskets are great for keeping envelopes, stationery, notepads, stamps, address book, and labels within arm's reach without cluttering up your work surface. This is especially useful if space is at a premium.

● An added basket bonus: If something spills—goopy hair gel, for example—the mess is confined to that one small basket. Less to clean up.

SHAKER PEGS OR SHAKER PEG RACKS

Available at most hardware and craft supply stores, these simple utilitarian devices can help restore order to chaos.

● Screw one into the back of closets to hang pocketbooks, knapsacks, scarves, frequently worn jackets, hats, and belts.

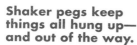

Shaker pegs keep things all hung up— and out of the way.

● A row of evenly spaced Shaker pegs on a garage wall makes the perfect place to hang garden tools: hoes, shovels, spades, etc. Before you screw in the pegs, line up all your tools. Use the longest-handled tool to help you determine how high the pegs should be hung.

● Do your kids leave wet towels all around the yard after swimming in the pool or running through the sprinkler? Hang some of these all-purpose pegs on the outside wall of a garage, shed, or side of the house. It's the perfect place to drape towels between dips. Towels stay cleaner longer because they're not tossed on the ground.

● A row of brightly painted Shaker pegs in a child's room makes a terrific place to hang bags of toys. Make sure you hang them low enough so little hands can help themselves.

● You can also use the pegs to hang kids' artwork. Loop a string from the top corners of paper creations, then suspend them from the pegs.

● Shaker pegs in a mud room are perfect for wet mittens and hats.

HANGING SHOE BAGS

Plastic shoe bags with several compartments can help you keep clutter to a minimum.

● Use a shoe bag to store winter woolies—hats, mittens, scarves—in a hall closet. Choose a shoe bag with clear plastic pockets so the contents are easily visible.

● If there's no room in your house for a dedicated sewing center, use a hanging shoe bag as your "portable" sewing room. Use pockets to store scissors, thread, needles, pins, binding tape, zippers, buttons, and any other related items. When you're ready to sit down and mend, bring the shoe bag to whatever room you're working in. You can use it in the same way to store crafts items.

● The separate, see-through compartments of a hanging shoe bag are ideal for sorting and storing costume jewelry and clothing accessories, such as scarves and belts. Because you can hang it in your clothes closet, everything is right there for you to see when you're getting dressed. Also, if you always wear a group of accessories together, pack them in one pocket. Getting out of the house in a hurry is that much easier.

● Use a hanging shoe bag as a mobile—and neat—activity center for the kids in the car. Simply hang one on the back of the driver's seat and one on the back of the front passenger's seat. Fill the bag with kid- and car-friendly items: paper, crayons, washable markers, stickers, small puzzles, coloring books, dry snacks. Kids sitting in the back seat can reach forward to help themselves.

The Sporting Life

● Heavy-duty plastic garbage pails with wheels attached make excellent storage bins for sports equipment. They're large, easy to move around, and can hold a lot. You can group equipment by season: spring—baseballs, bats, gloves, soccer balls, nets, cleats; summer—water skis, diving equipment, fins, masks, snorkels, life jackets, flotation devices; fall—basketballs, footballs, pads, helmets; winter—skis, boots, ice skates, hockey sticks, pucks, pads, masks.

Fill the see-through pockets of a hanging shoe bag with kid-friendly stuff for a portable play center.

CHAPTER 2

Paper Tamers

Do you find yourself being buried under an avalanche of paper each week? Advertising supplements, catalogs, bills, school notices—they all pile up quickly. With our roundup of paper-taming hints, you can easily dig yourself out from under the pile.

Whip those paper piles into shape or eliminate them altogether.

File That Under "J" for Junk

● Read the mail over a garbage pail or recycling bin and immediately discard unwanted advertisements, unsolicited mail, and catalogs *before* they turn into paper clutter in your house.

● If you think you might want to order something, immediately fill in and tear out the order form; discard the rest.

Paper Blockades

● Or remove your name from junk mail lists altogether. Write to Mail Preference Service, c/o Direct Marketing Association, P.O. Box 9008, Farmingdale, NY 11735-9008. Include your full name and address, as well as any variations on your name. This service also eliminates junk mail for people no longer living at your address.

● If you order an item by catalog, indicate on the order form (there's usually a box you can check off) or tell the salesperson on the phone that you do *not* want your name to be included on any list that's for rent or sale.

Systemize, Itemize, Economize

● Pick a spot in your home that will become "Paper Central"—a den, study, or maybe a desk area in the kitchen. This is where you'll keep the mail until you have time to look through it.

● Equip "Paper Central" with the following: an accordion-style folder with at least 12 pockets (one for each month), a file cabinet, stationery, pens, stamps, prepaid postcards, address book or circular address file, and return address labels or self-inking stamp.

One letter can put an end to unwanted junk mail.

- Use color-coded folders to create a family filing system: blue folders for kids' school papers, green folders for bills and financial documents, red for important papers. Have your children put their papers into the "School" folder when they get home, sort the mail into the appropriate folders, and you'll be able to find things easily.

- When you have time to look through the mail, concentrate on one folder at a sitting, but make sure you take action on everything in that folder. For example, if you are sorting through the "School" folder, sign or fill out whatever paperwork is there, then mail it or give it to your child to return to the teacher. Remember, try to handle each piece of paper as few times as necessary.

- Shift those papers that can't be dealt with immediately into a folder labeled

Paper Central: a place for every paper, and every paper in its place.

"Pending" or "Follow Up." Glance through this folder each time you sort through the mail as a reminder of what other information or action you need to take to be done with it.

- When a bill arrives, open it and put it in its return envelope along with a check. Write the due date on the outside of the envelope. In your accordion-style folder, file bills in the order they are due. Go through the folder once a week and mail the bills marked for that time.

- Buy greeting cards in bulk— stamp and address them, then file them in your accordion-style folder. On the first of each month, mail off your cards.

● Create a "To Read" basket for magazines and catalogs. Put scissors, paper clips, and sticky notes in the basket so that when you go through the stack you can clip, snip, or tag the pages you want to refer to again. Toss the leftovers.

Artful Options

● Inexpensive under-the-bed storage boxes come in a variety of colors and make great containers for your kids' special memory items. Choose a different color for each child.

Laminating kids' art puts it to practical use.

● If you can't find the refrigerator handle because the door is plastered with your kids' art projects, try this: Take their favorite drawings and paintings to a copy center and have them laminated. They make terrific place mats and crafts project mats. Your kids will be thrilled that their masterpieces have been preserved.

● Since the art projects your children bring home come in all shapes and sizes, buy a large portfolio case from any art supply store. After you've displayed a child's creation for a reasonable amount of time, store it in the folder. At the end of the school year, have your children pick out the one or two pieces they'd like to keep as their "masterpieces." Discard the rest.

● If your youngster brings home artwork that's covered with glitter or other messy, hard-to-clean-up pieces, enclose the project in a resealable plastic bag with a zipper-type lock, then hang it up.

All the News That's Fit to Reuse

It's amazing how quickly old newspapers stack up. Here's how to make them do double duty:

● Use newspapers as weed screens in your garden beds. Spread a few pages on the ground, hose them thoroughly with water, then put mulch or dirt on top. Pierce through the softened paper with a spade to set in your plants. The paper decomposes, so it won't hurt the environment, but it keeps weeds from poking through.

● Shredded newspaper makes a terrific mulch for vegetable garden beds.

● Use the Sunday comic section as gift wrapping paper. It's especially fun for children's presents.

● Roll papers tightly into 3-inch-diameter logs. They're great for starting campfires.

Recycle Pile

● Reuse junk mail envelopes to store your weekly grocery coupons. Write your shopping list on the outside of the envelope and put a star next to each item for which you have a coupon.

• Turn old greeting cards into postcards. Cut the card in half at the fold. The half with the image on it is usually blank on the other side. Draw a line down the center, write your greeting on one side, the address on the other. Stamp and mail.

• Do you have a box full of duplicate photo prints? Don't let them sit there gathering dust—turn them into postcards! Jot your note or greeting on the blank side, then mail it. Your family and friends not only get to read what you're up to but get a glimpse too!

• To keep sloppy stacks of newspapers, magazines, and cardboard neat until trash day, tie them up with an old pair of panty hose. The panty hose can stretch far enough to accommodate an oversize bundle, and they're sturdy enough to use as a handle to carry the bundle to the curb.

• Use the backs of unsolicited mail for scratch paper. Write lists or informal notes to school or friends.

Handle with Care

• Keep warranty information, receipts, and instruction manuals for appliances or electronic equipment together in resealable zipper-lock plastic bags. File them in your "Warranties" folder, or punch holes in the plastic bag so it fits into a binder that you can keep on a bookshelf.

Name Game

• Here's how to keep track of those hard-to-remember bank and other PIN numbers without accumulating a pile of paper reminders. Make them part of a fictitious telephone number in your address book. For example: Jane Doe, 123-4567.

Menu Venue

• A large manila envelope glued to the inside cover of the telephone book is a great place to keep take-out menus, pizza delivery coupons, and the like.

How Long Should You Keep It?

Here's a guide to what you must save and what can be tossed.

4 YEARS*	FOREVER	OTHER
✔ Bank statements ✔ Canceled checks ✔ Credit card statements, paid bills ✔ Records of sales of investments ✔ Utility bills if you're taking a home office deduction *The time during which the IRS can question your return	✔ Adoption records, birth certificates ✔ Death certificates ✔ Marriage certificate ✔ Divorce papers ✔ Medical records ✔ Military discharge ✔ Tax returns ✔ Vaccination records ✔ Receipts for permanent home improvements	✔ Paycheck stubs: until confirmed with W-2 at year's end ✔ Warranties: for as long as you own the product 

VIP List

Don't waste time scrambling through a variety of different phone books, Rolodexes, or index card files for the numbers you need. Make a copy of this page, fill it out, then duplicate it for every member of your family. Keep another copy in your house where it's accessible to all.

	NAME	ADDRESS/PHONE NUMBER
Doctors		
Allergist		
Chiropractor		
Dentist		
Family physician		
Ob/Gyn		
Optometrist		
Pediatrician		
Veterinarian		
Other		
Other		
Utilities		
Cable TV		
Electric		
Gas		
Oil		
Sanitation		
Telephone		
Water		
Other		

NAME	ADDRESS/PHONE NUMBER
Services	
AC/Heating	
Car care	
Electrician	
Pharmacist	
Plumber	
Yard service	
Other	
Financial	
Accountant	
Attorney	
Banker	
Financial planner	
Insurance agent	
Car	
Home	
Life	
Stockbroker	
Other	
Other	
Other	

Organize Electronically

The promise of a "paperless society" is still a long way off for most people, but advances in technology are definitely moving us in that direction.

● Now a computer and scanner are all you need to eliminate years of paper records. Remember to back up your files on disks so if your system crashes, you won't lose everything on your hard drive.

● Organize your e-mail address list by groups: family members, bowling team members, kids' playmates. Then, when you want to send a message relevant to a group, all the names you need are together. One e-mail keeps everyone up-to-date.

● Personal information managers (like the Palm Pilot) are the electronic equivalent of a Filofax. Keep track of schedules and create, categorize, and prioritize your to-do lists. Loaded into a handheld device, your schedules and lists travel with you. Then you can transfer the information to your PC without ever using a pen or paper.

Web Wonders

The Internet is the gateway to hundreds of resources, and the best part of it is that you can access the Web 24 hours a day, so you aren't constricted by store or library hours when you just have to find a recipe for *Schaumtorte* (German foam cake) or need to resolve all sorts of dilemmas.

● In addition to the Web sites listed here, GTE's superpages.com, **http://superpages.gte.net,** is a general site that offers a variety of consumer services, such as a virtual shopping mall, product ratings, a city guide, and a customized mapping feature.

● Narrow your online searches by putting the subject in quotes. For example, without quotes a search for Ancient Roman Government will yield everything with the words "Ancient," "Roman," or "Government," not just Ancient Roman Government.

How to Solve 15 of Life's Little Disasters—Fast!

1 **"I'm out of coffee, baby food, and diapers. I have the flu and can't leave the house."** Not to worry, NetGrocer, **www.netgrocer.com,** can take care of most of your shopping needs. The virtual supermarket has a selection of thousands of nonperishable products from such categories as Gourmet Foods, Baby & Kids, and Housewares, and boasts food prices 20 percent below supermarket costs. Groceries ship FedEx within one to four days and cost $2.99 for orders up to $50 and $4.99 for orders over $50.

2 **"My daughter has head lice— and a big wad of gum stuck in her hair."** ParentsPlace.com, **www.parentsplace.com,** offers all the information you need to know, from how to treat your children's colds or flu to what diseases you can get from pets. There's also expert advice on infertility, pregnancy, and breastfeeding and a link to iVillage.com, The Women's Network **(www.ivillage.com).**

3 *"My car is making strange gurgling sounds, smoke is coming out of the tailpipe, and I can see daylight through the floorboard. We're going on a family vacation next week, and I need a new car."* Car buying was never easier. Before making a trip to a showroom, take a virtual spin around the block at AutoSite, **www.autosite.com.** Its "AutoFinder" feature matches your car preferences to the latest makes and models. It also provides information on the latest rebates and incentives and lets you compare financing rates.

4 *"I'm getting married in two weeks, and my wedding dress never arrived from the factory!"* Planning a wedding can be an anxiety-producing experience. But before you run all over town looking for that perfect gown, flowers, and a photographer, sign on to The Knot, **www.theknot.com.** In addition to a database of over 8,000 bridal gowns, a gift registry, and beauty and etiquette tips, The Knot has a customizable budget planner to help couples determine the cost of their wedding.

5 *"My son has to figure out the radius of a 30-inch pizza—by tomorrow!"* No problem, just visit Ask Dr. Math, **www.forum. swarthmore.edu/dr.math/ dr-math.html,** a site staffed by college math students. Dr. Math answers questions from kids in kindergarten through grade 12. Questions are answered by e-mail; there is also an archive of problems searchable by topic.

6 *"My cat is so depressed, she just lies on the couch, ignoring me. Even catnip can't snap her out of it."* Want to know what's bugging your pet? At **www.pamperedcat.com,** you can pose your pussy cat question directly to a specialist veterinarian who treats only cats. Here you might also find the perfect toy to entice your kitty off the couch, or a delicious cat delicacy to tempt her palate.

7 *"I've been putting off getting the roof fixed, but I've run out of pans to hold the leaks."* Let ImproveNet, **www.improvenet.com,** help you solve your various home-improvement problems. This comprehensive site has links to a database of over 600,000 prescreened contractors and lists recommended architects and designers. You can even get free advice from ImproveNet experts. Just tell the site about your building problem, and it will locate and e-mail you the names of three to six prescreened contractors in your area within a week.

8 *"We just moved to a colder climate. Which outdoor plants will thrive here?"* GardenWeb, **www.gardenweb.com,** is a cornucopia of gardening delights. With more than 60 online forums, gardeners can discuss topics ranging from growing wildflowers and native plants to taking care of roses. The site also contains a glossary of botanical terms, a calendar of events in your area, and a bulletin board where gardeners can ask about hard-to-find seeds and plants.

9 "The furniture I recently bought is damaged, and the store won't take it back." Check out Consumer World, **www.consumerworld.org,** a one-stop shop for consumers complete with 1,700 resources. You can lodge complaints with a government or consumer affairs department, search for a low-rate credit card, shop for bargains, and get buying advice.

10 "The restaurant where I was the chef had a grease fire and burned down—oops." To find a new job, look no further than Monster.com, **www.monster.com.** This easy-to-use site has over 50,000 job listings worldwide, plus a "Résumé City" feature that helps you develop a résumé and then stores it in an employer-searchable database.

11 "My husband's company just transferred him to another state. We have to find a new house right away." Moving is always traumatic, but Coldwell Banker, **www.coldwellbanker.com,** can make finding a new home a lot easier. The site has 190,000 housing listings around the U.S. and parts of Canada. The "Neighborhood Explorer" feature provides details of specific neighborhoods, including school systems and housing prices.

12 "My parents are opera fans. I'd love to get them tickets for their anniversary, but I don't know what events are scheduled in their city." For up-to-date listings of over 200,000 theater, opera, dance, and film events taking place all across the country, log on to CultureFinder.com, **www.culturefinder.com.** This site allows you to browse by state and city, lists performance times, and even gives event recommendations. You can order your tickets online or through an 800 number.

13 "I have to go out of town on a business trip. I'm a vegetarian and I'm watching my weight." No matter what your food preference is, **www.zagat.com,** the ZAGAT Survey Web site, will help you find a restaurant to suit you. This site, based on the printed version of ZAGAT guides, lists U.S. eateries by city, cuisine, food ranking, and price range.

14 "Yikes! My mother-in-law's birthday is tomorrow, and I forgot to mail her a card." You can get out of the doghouse fast by logging on to Blue Mountain Arts, **www.bluemountain.com,** and e-mailing her a personalized card. This free greeting-card site has a large variety of fun, animated cards suitable for any occasion, from birthday and anniversary to Mother-in-Law's Day and National Dog Week.

15 "It's midnight, and the pain in my foot is back." To find health information, log on to healthfinder, **www.healthfinder.gov.** This versatile site, developed by the Department of Health and Human Services, has links to over 3,200 medical sites, including publications, searchable databases, support and self-help groups, government agencies, and nonprofit organizations.

Easy Meal and Party Planning

"**W**hat's for dinner?" "What did you give me for lunch?" "Quick, company's coming—what do we have to serve?" If these scenarios make you want to run for the hills, relax. The hints in this chapter will help ease some of the pressure, from how to negotiate through the grocery store faster to what to have on hand to make it easy to impress your guests—even when they drop in unexpectedly.

A sit-down dinner for 12? No problem. Just follow our party-planning time line.

Shop Smart

● For quick grocery shopping, make an aisle-by-aisle list and photocopy it. Each week just circle the items on the list that you need to replenish your pantry. If you have coupons, note them on the list next to the item.

● Or if your supermarket has printed up a comprehensive store directory, you may want to try this: Cover a copy of the directory with transparent adhesive plastic or take it to a copy center and have it laminated. What you've got is a reusable shopping list. Use a grease pencil to circle the items you need for that week, then erase the markings after you've shopped. With the list posted in your kitchen—on the refrigerator with a magnet, for example—anyone in your family can circle needed items as the week goes by.

Presorting and bagging your own groceries saves time when you unpack.

● To make putting your groceries away easier, bag them yourself at the supermarket so you can group items together the way they are stored in your kitchen.

Salad Bar Supper

● When you need to make dinner in a hurry, the supermarket salad bar is a great place to buy precleaned and cut-up vegetables. You can throw some broccoli and carrots into a pot of cooking pasta and top with a salad dressing for a quick "primavera," or stir-fry vegetables in a skillet or wok with chicken or beef strips or precleaned shrimp.

All Steamed Up

● Here's an easy way to steam vegetables: Put them in a resealable plastic bag (leave a small opening for the steam to escape), add a bit of water, and place in the microwave. Cook for 2 to 3 minutes or until tender.

Good-Looking Fruit

● Keep apple and banana slices from turning brown by placing them on a plate containing a small amount of a lemon-lime soft drink.

● Another lemony option: Fill a small spray bottle with lemon juice and keep it in the refrigerator. Use it to lightly spray cut-up fruit to keep it from darkening and cooked vegetables and salads to give them extra tang.

Dill-icious

● If you have leftover steamed vegetables, put them in a jar of leftover dill pickle juice and refrigerate. In a day or two, the vegetables will absorb the juice. For a quick dinner, cook and drain pasta and toss with the marinated vegetables. This is also great for tossing in salads or with canned tuna fish.

● For a flavorful and easy way to make coleslaw, potato salad, or macaroni salad, substitute pickle juice for the vinegar. You won't need to add any other seasonings.

Rice and Easy

● You can save meal preparation time by cooking rice in advance. Here's how: In a covered bowl, combine 1 cup dry rice, 2 cups water, and a pinch of salt. Cook for an hour in an oven heated to 350 degrees. After the rice cools, place it in the refrigerator or freezer to use later in stir-fry recipes, casseroles, puddings, and other dishes.

Shelving Dinner

● Working mothers usually have to do a lot of preplanning. One way to help you get dinner started quickly when you get home is to keep the cans, boxes, and containers you need for one recipe together on the same shelf. For example, group the jarred spaghetti sauce, pasta box, and canned mushrooms together.

Leftover Magic

● Don't throw away those limp outer leaves from a head of lettuce. You can use them to cover food that's to be reheated in the microwave. The lettuce leaves preserve the food's moistness and flavor.

● Uneaten garlic bread can be frozen and then grated to make tasty seasoned bread crumbs for coating chicken, chops, and vegetables.

● Combine the last bits of cold cereal from several boxes into one airtight resealable container. Not only does this free up some cabinet space, but it also makes for a new, one-of-a-kind breakfast cereal.

Cereal's never the same when you create your own "mixed bag" from boxes' last bits.

How Long Will It Keep?

Write the date food went into your freezer using an indelible marker on the outside of freezer bags or on masking tape affixed to freezer paper. For refrigerated food, put older purchases toward the front of the fridge, just-bought items toward the back. If you still have raw eggs left from the previous week's shopping, write on the outside of the shell, "Use first."

FOOD	REFRIGERATE	FREEZE
Meat (Raw)		
Beef steaks/roasts	1 to 2 days	6 to 12 months
Ground beef, veal, lamb, stew	1 to 2 days	3 to 4 months
Ground pork	1 to 2 days	1 to 3 months
Lamb chops/steaks/roasts	1 to 2 days	6 to 9 months
Organ meats	1 to 2 days	3 to 4 months
Pork chops	1 to 2 days	3 to 4 months
Pork sausages	1 to 2 days	1 to 2 months
Veal cutlets	1 to 2 days	6 to 9 months
Veal steaks	1 to 2 days	6 to 12 months
Poultry (Raw)		
Chicken, cut-up	1 to 2 days	9 months
Chicken, whole	1 to 2 days	12 months
Chicken giblets	1 to 2 days	3 months
Duck or goose, whole	1 to 2 days	6 months
Turkey, whole/cut-up	1 to 2 days	6 months
Fish (Raw)		
Fresh fish	1 to 2 days	6 to 9 months
Shrimp	1 to 2 days	2 months
Lobster, crabs	1 to 2 days	1 to 2 months (shelled)
Oysters, clams, scallops	1 to 2 days	3 to 6 months (shelled)
Cooked Meat/Poultry/Fish		
Beef roast/stew	3 to 4 days	2 to 3 months
Chicken, fried	1 to 2 days	4 months
Chicken pieces in broth/gravy	1 to 2 days	6 months
Chicken pieces not in broth/gravy	1 to 2 days	1 month
Chicken/tuna salad	1 to 2 days	do not freeze
Fish	2 to 3 days	1 month
Fresh ham/pork	3 to 4 days	2 to 3 months
Meat broth/gravy	1 to 2 days	2 to 3 months
Meat loaf	2 to 3 days	3 months
Meat spaghetti sauce	3 to 4 days	6 to 8 months
Pork or lamb	3 to 4 days	2 to 3 months

FOOD	REFRIGERATE	FREEZE
Cured Meats		
Bacon	1 week	2 to 4 months
Corned beef	1 week	2 weeks
Frankfurters	1 week	1 month
Ham, canned (unopened)	1 year	do not freeze
Ham, whole	1 week	1 to 2 months
Luncheon meat	3 to 5 days	do not freeze
Sausage, smoked	7 days	do not freeze
Dairy Products		
Butter, salted	2 weeks	3 months
Butter, unsalted	2 weeks	6 months
Cheese, hard	2 to 3 months	6 months
Cheese, soft	2 weeks	2 months
Cottage cheese	5 to 7 days	1 to 2 weeks
Cream cheese	2 weeks	2 weeks
Egg, whole	2 to 3 days	do not freeze
Egg whites	2 to 3 days	12 days
Egg yolks	2 to 3 days	do not freeze
Milk, cream	1 week	6 months
Fruits		
Apples	1 month	1 year
Apricots, avocados, bananas, grapes, melons, nectarines, peaches, pears, pineapples, plums	3 to 5 days	1 year
Berries, cherries	2 to 3 days	1 year
Citrus fruits	2 weeks	1 year
Cranberries	1 week	1 year
Vegetables		
Asparagus	2 to 3 days	6 months
Broccoli, Brussels sprouts, lima beans, rhubarb, green onions, spinach, summer squash	3 to 5 days	6 months
Cabbage	1 to 2 weeks	6 months
Carrots, beets, parsnips, turnips	2 weeks	6 months
Cauliflower, celery, green beans, peppers, cucumbers, tomatoes	1 week	6 months
Lettuce, salad greens	1 week	do not freeze

Nice Spice

● If your powdered spices and seasonings become clumpy, lumpy, and difficult to pour during high heat and humidity, here's a way to keep them fresh: Store them in the door of your refrigerator's freezer compartment.

Box Lunch

● To keep sandwiches made with soft white or wheat bread from getting smashed, try this: Slide the individually wrapped sandwich inside an empty four-stick butter or margarine box. It's the perfect size for one sandwich, and the box still fits nicely into a brown bag, lunch box, or briefcase.

● Make, wrap, and freeze a stack of peanut butter (and jelly) sandwiches at the beginning of the week to toss in lunch bags as needed.

Bag It!

● Once a week, use sandwich-size plastic bags to convert large, economy-size bags of chips, cookies, nuts, dried fruits, raisins, and other goodies into single-size servings. Store the bags in a large sealed container. When it's time to fix lunches, toss the prepared bag into the lunch box along with a sandwich and fruit. This really saves time in the morning—especially if you have to fix several lunches each day. Making your own individual snack bags saves you money too.

Portion Control

● Do you purchase ice cream by the half-gallon and find that your kids eat more than a single portion? Put single servings into empty yogurt containers and freeze.

Party-Planning Primer

Be a guest at your own party. The key is careful preparation and timing.

4 Weeks Ahead	3 Weeks Ahead	2 Weeks Ahead	1 Week Ahead
● Decide what kind of party you want (dinner, buffet, potluck). ● Make a guest list. ● Write a to-do list. ● Book a caterer and arrange for rentals if necessary. (During holidays, contact the caterer at least a month ahead; six weeks is even better.)	● Invite your guests. Allow one week for the invitations to arrive by mail. During the busy holiday season, invite guests extra early.	● Finalize your menu. ● Draft a shopping list of everything you'll need, from food to candles to bathroom tissues. Confirm the caterer if applicable. ● Purchase the groceries for make-ahead recipes. Prepare and freeze whatever you can.	● Buy all the nonperishables, including liquor, wine, soda, mixers, flour, sugar, canned goods, aluminum foil, plastic cups, and paper towels.

Here's another way to preportion ice cream from large containers into single servings: Fill a muffin pan with paper cupcake holders. Put one scoop of ice cream into each cup, freeze, then repackage in resealable plastic bags.

● Or make graham cracker ice cream sandwiches. First break the graham crackers into squares, then fill with softened ice cream, wrap individually, and freeze.

● Need to frost just-baked cupcakes in a hurry? Place a miniature chocolate candy bar on top of each cupcake. Spread the chocolate evenly as it melts.

● Store cookie, cracker, and cereal crumbs in airtight containers to use as sprinkles on top of ice cream or yogurt.

● For a quick, easy, and oh-so-sweet frosting, add a little maple syrup to confectioners' sugar and stir until thick. Spread on cakes, cookies, or buns.

Tip-top Toppings

● For variety—and to give pancakes and waffles an extra-flavorful and healthful boost—heat up some fruit-only preserves and use as a substitute for syrup. Warmed-up preserves also make a delicious topping for ice cream.

Warmed-up fruit preserves or jams are a deliciously different topping for pancakes.

1–3 Days Ahead	1 Day Ahead	2–8 Hours Ahead	1 Hour Ahead
● Clean and decorate the house. ● Make extra room in your refrigerator. ● Prepare any recipes that can be made fully or partially this far in advance. ● Confirm again with the caterer and rental company. You can never do this too often.	● Cook all food that can possibly be prepared now. ● Remove all prepared food from the freezer; thaw overnight in the refrigerator. ● Double-check your list to make sure you have everything you need. ● If displaying flowers, buy and arrange.	● Set the table. ● Position the centerpiece. ● Gather all serving pieces and set nearby. ● Prepare any dishes that don't require a lot of last-minute attention. ● Arrange any platters of food that will be served cold.	● Get dressed and rest. ● Quickly survey the table arrangements, beverages, and food; make any minor last-minute adjustments as needed. ● Add any needed garnishes to food. ● Put out any foods that are to be served at room temperature. ● Line up appropriate musical selections so they're ready to play. ● Empty the dishwasher.

Squeeze Please

● Depending upon size, one whole lemon yields between 2½ and 3½ tablespoons juice.

● To double the amount of juice you can get from a citrus fruit, hold the fruit under warm water before squeezing.

Brown Bag Special

● Here's a quick way to make a low-calorie snack: Place ¼ cup popcorn in a brown paper lunch bag. Fold the top over a few times. Place the bag on its side and microwave on high until the popping slows.

In-a-Pinch Substitutions

It happens to the best of us. You're halfway through a recipe and you discover you don't have an ingredient you need. Take heart—all is not lost. You can make these switches and your recipe will be saved.

RECIPE CALLS FOR	YOU MAY SUBSTITUTE
1 square unsweetened chocolate	3 tablespoons unsweetened cocoa + 1 tablespoon butter/margarine
1 cup cake flour	1 cup less 2 tablespoons all-purpose flour
2 tablespoons flour (for thickening)	1 tablespoon cornstarch
1 tablespoon baking powder	¼ teaspoon baking soda + 1 teaspoon cream of tartar + ¼ teaspoon cornstarch
1 cup corn syrup	1 cup sugar + ¼ cup additional liquid used in recipe
1 cup milk	½ cup evaporated milk + ½ cup water
1 cup buttermilk or sour milk	1 tablespoon vinegar or lemon juice + enough milk to make 1 cup
1 cup sour cream (for baking)	1 cup plain yogurt
1 cup firmly packed brown sugar	1 cup sugar + 2 tablespoons molasses
1 teaspoon lemon juice	¼ teaspoon vinegar (not balsamic)
¼ cup chopped onion	1 tablespoon instant minced onion
1 clove garlic	¼ teaspoon garlic powder
1 cup tomato juice	½ cup tomato sauce + ½ cup water
2 cups tomato sauce	¾ cup tomato paste + 1 cup water
1 tablespoon prepared mustard	1 teaspoon dry mustard + 1 tablespoon water
1 tablespoon fresh snipped herbs	1 teaspoon dried herbs

Cupcake Cones

● For a neat, complete, eat-it-all treat, fill flat-bottomed ice cream cones two-thirds full with cupcake batter and bake on a cookie sheet. After they've cooled, add frosting and sprinkles. Especially fun for a kids' party.

Sweet Somethings

● Crush leftover hard candy and add it to chocolate chip cookie batter, ice cream sundaes, cake frosting, and the like.

Chef's Shortcut

● To crush fresh ginger quickly and easily, peel the ginger and force it through a garlic press.

● To cut dried fruits, marshmallows, or gumdrops, dip kitchen scissors frequently into hot water.

A-Peeling Idea

● To peel a non-navel orange or a tomato cleanly, dunk it in hot water for a minute or two, then into cold water for the same amount of time. Presto! An easy-to-peel orange or tomato.

No-More-Tears Onions

● To practically eliminate onion odor, store onions in the refrigerator for up to 24 hours before using them. After 24 hours you can cut the onions without shedding a single tear.

● If your eyes sting when you peel onions, light a candle and place it on the kitchen counter before you start to peel. The flame dispels the gas given off by the onion.

Entertaining Do's and Don'ts

DO...	DON'T...
● ask invited guests about any dietary restrictions. ● have someone behind the table to serve at a large buffet. Otherwise, before too long the food display will look like the day after a huge white sale. ● expect the unexpected; have extra food and place settings ready in case someone brings a surprise guest. ● use your best china, silver, and stemware for fancy dinner parties. After all, what do you have it for?	● set the bar and the buffet next to each other, or you'll create a bottleneck. ● experiment on your guests by making dishes that you've never made before. That's what family is for. ● use scented candles; they'll detract from the flavor of the food. ● delay dinner for latecomers— it's not fair to your other guests, not to mention the effect it will have on your food. ● apologize for your food, even if it hasn't come out quite right. Most people won't ever know the difference.

Better Biscuits

● Instead of rolling out biscuit dough, then cutting the dough into individual biscuits, spoon the dough into a muffin pan. There's less mess, and the biscuits are the same size and shape every time.

Cool Solution

● Keep a cooler in the trunk of your car to store perishables—milk, eggs, cheese—that might go bad if you can't get home immediately after shopping.

Baker's Secrets

● To cream butter and sugar quickly, rinse the bowl with boiling water first.

● Avoid wasting flour and keep your baking area neat and clean at the same time. Leave a brand-new powder puff in your flour canister to dust the pastry board.

When a dusting of flour is all you need, a powder puff does the trick.

● Line your measuring cup with flour before measuring out the molasses for your next holiday cookie recipe. The molasses pours out of the cup easily, and cleanup is really a snap.

● Whenever you buy a 5-pound bag of flour, place 1-cup measures of it in large resealable plastic sandwich or storage bags and store them in a cool, dry place. You can do the same with granulated sugar. Then when a recipe calls for a cup of flour or sugar, you just pull out the one or two bags you need.

● For an extra-special batch of pancakes, substitute flavored coffee creamer for half of the milk that's called for in the recipe.

● Store your rolling pin in the freezer. It's easier to roll out pie crusts and pastry dough with a frozen rolling pin.

● To get more meringue from egg whites, before beating add 2 teaspoons cold water for each egg white.

● Don't worry if your homemade frosting isn't as thick as you'd like. Dust a little bit of flour or cornstarch on the cake first, then ice it. The frosting won't run.

● Whipped cream will stay fluffy and hold up longer if you mix it with a bit of confectioners' sugar.

● For great-tasting homemade apple pie every time, dust the pie pan with ground cinnamon.

No-Dud Spuds

● Freeze the leftover wrappers from sticks of butter or margarine. They're great to wrap around scrubbed potatoes before enclosing them in aluminum foil for baking. This adds just the right amount of buttery flavor and makes for a soft, delicious skin.

● To make mashed potatoes extra white and creamy, add scalded milk and beat well.

● Substitute low-fat chicken broth for milk and butter to make leaner mashed potatoes.

Sugar Substitute

● Use jarred baby fruit to flavor homemade cakes, cupcakes, and brownies. Baby fruit is a low-fat alternative to sugar, so when jars are on sale, stock up.

Hidden Vegetables

● A sneaky and tasty way to get your kids to eat their vegetables is to add jarred baby vegetables to some of your recipes. Stir a jar or two of carrots into a tomato sauce, or mix a jar of green beans and carrots into the meat loaf mix.

Neater Beater

● If you are using a handheld mixer, put the mixing bowl in the sink before you start to mix the batter. Spatters will be contained, and cleanup is a breeze.
● Before you use the food processor to grate cheese, coat the inside with vegetable cooking spray. It keeps the cheese from sticking to the blade.

Grease Relief

● Want to keep fried foods from spattering grease all over your stove? Next time, invert a metal colander over the frying pan. Steam escapes through the holes so food fries up nice and crisp, but spatters don't.

Hold a Candle to It

● To keep birthday candles upright on the cake, use lifesaver-shaped hard candy as the candleholders. They are a colorful—and edible—addition to the cake.
● Mini marshmallows also make nifty candleholders. The marshmallows keep the candle wax from dripping on the icing.
● Dining by candlelight? Store candles in the refrigerator. They will burn longer and drip less.

Easy 7-Day Dinner Plan

MENU	TIPS
Sunday Roast chicken Potatoes Vegetables Salad	● Roast a large chicken or turkey on Sunday, a day when there's time to spend in the kitchen.
Monday Chicken soup Rolls Salad	● Make chicken soup with the leftovers on Monday.
Tuesday Meat loaf Rice Salad	● On Tuesday, while preparing meat loaf, also make meat sauce for Wednesday's pasta dinner.
Wednesday Pasta with meat sauce Salad	● On Saturday there's leftover lasagna for the kids; adults dine out.
Thursday Vegetable lasagna Salad	● If you have unexpected leftovers, incorporate them on your weekly menu plan, on a day when cooking is out of the question. This way the leftovers get used and don't get stuck in the back of the fridge to be tossed out weeks later.
Friday Flounder Lentil and bean salad Vegetables	
Saturday Dine out (Leftover lasagna for the kids)	

Cheese Guide

CHEESE	HOW IT LOOKS AND TASTES	HOW TO SERVE
American, Cheddar	Favorite all-around cheeses. Flavor varies from mild to sharp. Color ranges from natural to yellow-orange; texture from firm to crumbly.	Use in sandwiches, casseroles, soufflés, and creamy sauces. Serve with fruit pie or crisp crackers, or on a snack or dessert tray with fruit.
Blue, Gorgonzola, Roquefort	Compact, creamy cheeses veined with blue or blue-green mold. Sometimes crumbly. Mild to sharp, salty flavor. (Stilton is similar, but like a blue-veined Cheddar.)	Crumble in salads, salad dressings, and dips. Delicious with fresh pears or apples for dessert. Blend with butter for steak topper. Spread on crackers or crusty French or Italian bread.
Brick	Medium firm; creamy yellow color, tiny holes. Flavor very mild to medium sharp.	Good for appetizers, sandwiches, or desserts. Great with fresh peaches, cherries, or melons.
Brie	Similar to Camembert, but slightly firmer. Distinctive sharp flavor, pronounced odor.	Serve as dessert with fresh fruit. Be sure to eat the thin brown and white crust.
Camembert	Creamy yellow with thin gray-white crust. When ripe, it softens to the consistency of thick cream. Full, rich, mildly pungent.	Classic dessert cheese. Serve at room temperature with fresh peaches, pears, or apples, or with toasted walnuts and crackers.
Cottage	Soft, mild, unripened cheese; large or small curd. May have cream added.	Use in salads, dips, and main dishes. Popular with fresh and canned fruits.
Cream	Very mild-flavored soft cheese with buttery texture. Rich and smooth. Available whipped and in flavored spreads.	Adds richness and body to molded and frozen salads, cheesecake, dips, frostings, or sandwich spreads. Serve whipped with dessert.
Edam, Gouda	Round, wax-coated cheeses; creamy yellow to yellow-orange inside; firm and smooth. Mild nutlike flavor.	Bright hub for dessert or snack trays. Good in sandwiches or crunchy salads or with crackers. Great with grapes and oranges.
Feta (sheep's or goat's)	Crumbly; white, salty. Lower in fat than most cow's milk cheese. (Soak in cold water and drain to remove some of the salt.)	Add to salads. Toss with hot pasta, olive oil, and black olives for a quick entrée.

CHEESE	HOW IT LOOKS AND TASTES	HOW TO SERVE
Havarti (cream enriched)	Buttery. May be flavored with dill or caraway.	Good on deli trays and crackers.
Liederkranz, Limburger	Robust flavor and highly aromatic. Soft and smooth when ripe. Liederkranz is milder in flavor and golden yellow in color. Limburger is creamy white.	Spread on pumpernickel, rye, or crackers. Team with apples, pears, and Tokay grapes. Serve as snack with salty pretzels and coffee.
Monterey Jack	Wheel or block. Light yellow. Mild semisoft to hard (depends on aging).	Mexican dishes and casseroles.
Mozzarella, Scamorze	Unripened. Mild-flavored and slightly firm. Creamy white to pale yellow.	Cooking cheese. A "must" for pizza and lasagna; good in toasted sandwiches and hot snacks.
Muenster	Between brick and Limburger. Mild to mellow flavor, creamy white. Medium hard, tiny holes.	Use in sandwiches or on snack or dessert trays. Good with fresh sweet cherries and melon wedges.
Neufchâtel (whole or skim)	White, soft, and creamy. Mild, slightly tangy.	Use in salads, sandwiches, and desserts. Good substitute for cream cheese.
Parmesan, Romano	Sharp, piquant, very hard cheeses. Come grated in shakers. (Parmesan is also available shredded.) Or grate your own.	Sprinkle on pizza, main dishes, breads, salads, and soups. Shake over buttered popcorn.
Port du Salut	Semisoft, smooth, and buttery. Mellow to robust flavor between Cheddar and Limburger.	Dessert cheese—delicious with fresh fruit; great with apple pie. Good for a snack tray.
Processed cheeses	Blends of fresh and aged natural cheeses, pasteurized and packaged. Smooth and creamy; melt easily. May be flavored.	Ideal for cheese sauces, soufflés, grilled cheese sandwiches, and casseroles. Handy for the snack tray too.
Ricotta	Mild, sweet, nutlike flavor. Soft, moist texture with loose curds.	Use in salads, lasagna, and desserts.
Swiss	Firm, pale yellow cheese, with large round holes. Sweet nutlike flavor.	Good in salads and sauces, or as a snack.

Lunch Bunch

● To spice up at-home lunches for kids, serve egg, tuna, or chicken salad in an ice cream cone rather than between two slices of bread. Kids think they're getting a "dessert" for lunch.

● In order to save money—and time—try organizing a lunch "cooperative" at your office. This is how it works: Find a group of like-minded people who usually eat in at lunch or who want to. Each week it's someone's turn to make lunch for the entire group. That means, with eight people in a group, you have to supply lunch only one week out of every two months. You receive a free lunch the other seven weeks. What a deal.

Use a turkey baster to make perfect pancakes every time.

Preventing Oil Spills

● A thoroughly cleaned squeeze-type syrup bottle is an ideal container for cooking oil. The bottle is easy to handle, and there are no messy drips and spills to clean up.

● Wrap a terry-cloth ponytail holder around a bottle of cooking oil to absorb the dripping oil that leaves a greasy ring on shelves.

Mock-amole

● To make a low-cal alternative to guacamole dip, dice half an avocado and add it to a bowl of salsa. Delicious!

Pancake Perfection

● For perfectly shaped pancakes or crêpes every time, use a meat baster to suck the batter up from the bowl and squeeze onto the hot griddle.

Microwave Cooking Basics

Your microwave can be used not only for making popcorn and reheating leftovers but for melting butter or chocolate, warming syrup, softening ice cream, heating fast food, cooking main dishes, and much more.

● There are browning grills, roasting racks, muffin pans, and other utensils made for microwaves. But begin with what you have.

GLASS

● Ovenproof glass or ceramic baking dishes in a variety of sizes are the most useful pans. Be sure glass, china, or pottery has no metal trim or signature on the bottom.

PLASTIC

● Dishwasher-safe plastic utensils and hard plastic dishes may be used in microwaves for short periods of time.

Foam cups and dishes and plastic baby bottles are safe for heating but should not be used for prolonged periods because melting may occur when the contents get boiling hot. Use plastic wrap as a covering, but pierce it before taking the dish out of the microwave to prevent steam burns.

PAPER

● Paper cups, plates, and towels should be used only for heating or defrosting. Long periods of microwaving may cause paper to burn. Wax paper can be used as a cover during cooking.

METAL

● In general, metal should not be used in your microwave. Microwaves cannot pass through metal, and food will only cook from the top. TV dinner trays less than ¾-inch deep are allowable because they are shallow enough for the microwave to penetrate and cook food from the top.

● Metal skewers can be used when the amount of food is much greater than the amount of metal, as in a filled kabob. Small pieces of foil can be used for shielding parts that are cooking too quickly.

OTHER MATERIALS

● Straw baskets, wooden spoons, and rubber spatulas can be used in the microwave for short periods of time.

WHAT TO DO

● When in doubt, always consult your microwave manual for advice on cooking techniques and equipment. Here are three basic concepts that apply to all foods:

Quantity Determines cooking time.

Measure for Measure

MEASURE	EQUALS
Teaspoons	
Under ⅛ teaspoon	Dash or pinch
1½ teaspoons	½ tablespoon
3 teaspoons	1 tablespoon
Tablespoons	
1 tablespoon	3 teaspoons
4 tablespoons	¼ cup
5⅓ tablespoons	⅓ cup
8 tablespoons	½ cup
10⅔ tablespoons	⅔ cup
16 tablespoons	1 cup
Cups	
¼ cup	4 tablespoons
⅓ cup	5⅓ tablespoons
½ cup	8 tablespoons
½ cup	¼ pint
⅔ cup	10⅔ tablespoons
1 cup	16 tablespoons
1 cup	½ pint
2 cups	1 pint
4 cups	1 quart
Liquid Measures	
2 tablespoons	1 fluid ounce
3 tablespoons	1 jigger
¼ cup	2 fluid ounces
½ cup	4 fluid ounces
1 cup	8 fluid ounces

Small amounts of food or liquid take less cooking time than larger amounts of the same ingredient.

Density Dense, heavy foods take longer to microwave than lighter foods because microwaves cannot penetrate as deeply and the food must heat by conduction from the hot outer edges.

Starting temperature Room temperature food cooks faster than food that is refrigerated. And refrigerated food cooks faster than frozen food.

10 Quick-Fix Pantry Items

With these items on hand, you can whip up something special on the spur of the moment:

1. ANCHOVY PASTE

A dab is all you need to give food a lift. ● Combine 1 stick softened butter, 2 tablespoons chopped fresh parsley, 1 tablespoon anchovy paste, and 1 tablespoon fresh tarragon. Roll up in plastic wrap and freeze. Place a pat of flavored butter on just-grilled fish. ● Toast slices of bread. Lightly spread with anchovy paste. Top with chopped tomatoes, chopped fresh basil, and a touch of vinegar for a speedy starter. Garnish with a basil leaf.

2. CAPERS

Rinse salted capers lightly before using; use those packed in vinegar straight from the jar. ● Accent pasta by adding 2 tablespoons mashed capers and 2 tablespoons chopped black olives to 2 cups chunky marinara sauce. Toss with 1 pound cooked spaghetti. ● Mix ¼ cup low-fat mayonnaise, ¼ cup sour cream, 2 teaspoons lemon juice, 1 tablespoon mashed capers, and 1 tablespoon chopped fresh dill for a tasty tartar sauce.

3. DRIED FRUITS

Apricots, dates, and other dried fruits

Kitchen Metric Conversions

Liters, cups? Ounces, grams? Use this chart to help you convert one measurement to the other.

TO CHANGE	TO	MULTIPLY BY	METRIC UNITS IN DAILY LIVING
Ounces (oz.)	Grams (g)	28	● A dash of salt is about 1ml.
Pounds (lb.)	Kilograms (kg)	.45	● A quart of milk is just less than 1l.
Fluid ounces	Milliliters (ml)	30	● A paper clip weighs about 1g.
Cups (c.)	Liters (l)	.24	● The thickness of a dime is 1 millimeter (mm).
Quarts (qt.)	Liters (l)	.95	● 1 inch is equivalent to 2.5 centimeters (cm).
Gallons (gal.)	Liters (l)	3.8	● Water freezes at 0 degree Celsius.
Farenheit degrees (F)	Celsius degrees (C)	⅝ after subtracting 32	● Room temperature is 20 to 25 degrees Celsius.

add both flavor and texture. ● Give baked chicken a Moroccan twist: Season 1 cut-up chicken with 1 teaspoon ground cinnamon and ½ teaspoon ground cumin. Combine 1 sliced onion, 2 sliced carrots, 4 chopped dried apricots, and 4 chopped dates. Place the chicken, ½ cup broth, and the fruit-vegetable mixture in a baking dish. Bake in a preheated 350-degree oven 45 minutes or until the chicken is cooked. ● When making couscous, add ½ cup chopped dried fruits along with the water. When the couscous is ready, add 2 tablespoons pine nuts.

4. ITALIAN DRESSING

More than just a salad topper, it can be used as a marinade or glaze for meats. ● Mix equal parts Italian salad dressing and apricot jam; brush on pork tenderloin. Grill or bake, brushing occasionally during cooking. ● For an easy side dish, quarter or halve 1 pound cleaned white button mushrooms. Simmer in water to cover until tender, about 10 minutes. Drain well, then toss with ⅓ cup dressing. Refrigerate 2 hours before serving. ● Fast German potato salad: Boil 2 pounds unpeeled red potatoes. When they are tender, cut them in half. Combine with 3 slices cooked bacon, chopped, and ½ cup dressing mixed with 2 tablespoons sugar.

Grated Parmesan adds zest to pureed black beans for a zingy dip.

Sprinkle chopped parsley on top. Toss; let stand briefly or refrigerate a few hours to blend the flavors.

5. MARINATED ARTICHOKES

Put the marinade, as well as the artichoke, to good use. ● Pasta in no time: Chop the artichokes from 1 small jar; combine with 2 chopped ripe tomatoes. Stir in the marinade; let the flavors meld while cooking ½ pound pasta. The sauce will "cook" when tossed with the drained hot pasta. ● Give sautéed chicken legs extra oomph by adding a small jar of drained artichokes, cut in quarters, to 8 chicken legs during the last 15 minutes of cooking. ● For a Greek feast: Top focaccia with 1 small jar drained, quartered artichoke hearts, ¼ pound crumbled feta cheese, and 1 cup halved cherry tomatoes. Heat briefly.

6. OLIVES

● Top 4 baked potatoes with a mix of ½ cup light sour cream, 3 chopped green onions, 2 tablespoons chopped pimientos, and 2 tablespoons minced olives. ● Sauté 1 diced red bell pepper, 1 diced green bell pepper, 1 diced red onion, ½ cup diced olives, and ½ teaspoon crushed fennel seeds in a nonstick skillet until tender. Season with a splash of vinegar. Serve with smoked turkey breast.

7. PARMESAN

● For a southwestern dip, puree a 16-ounce can drained black beans. Add ¼ cup grated Parmesan cheese, 1 teaspoon ground cumin, 1 teaspoon dried oregano, and a dash of hot sauce; stir.

● Dip 4 chicken cutlets in a mix of 2 beaten eggs, ¼ cup grated Parmesan, 1 teaspoon dried basil, and a pinch of dried red pepper flakes. Bake at 350 degrees until cooked through.

8. PESTO

Make pesto fresh from basil, garlic, pine nuts, and olive oil during the summer. Off season, pick up a jar for a taste of summer anytime.

● Jazz up simple fish fillets: On each fillet, spread a teaspoon of pesto and bake. Just before the fish is done, sprinkle with freshly grated sharp cheese. ● To make omelets festive, fill them with pesto mixed with cooked chopped vegetables or shredded Monterey Jack cheese. Easy!

9. ROASTED RED PEPPER

● Perk up shrimp: Whirl ½ cup red pepper strips, 2 cloves garlic, ½ cup chopped fresh parsley, and 1 tablespoon lemon juice in a food processor or blender. Brush on cleaned shrimp. Bake at 350 degrees about 10 minutes, until cooked through. ● For a Tex-Mex side dish with Mediterranean flair: Cook 1½ cups rice in 3 cups broth. When the rice is just about cooked, stir in ½ cup chopped pepper strips and ¾ cup frozen corn; season with ½ teaspoon dried oregano and

½ teaspoon ground cumin. Cover and cook until the corn is tender.

10. SUN-DRIED TOMATOES

Sun-dried tomatoes enhance many types of dishes.

Soften dry-pack dried tomatoes for 10 minutes in hot water before using. For dried tomatoes packed in oil, pat off the excess before using. ● Italian-style quesadillas: Place 2 tablespoons shredded mozzarella cheese, 1 teaspoon chopped dried tomatoes, and 1 tablespoon minced fresh basil on an 8-inch flour tortilla; top with a second tortilla. Bake until the cheese melts.

● Impressive appetizer: Brush a pizza shell very lightly with olive oil. Cut 8 dried tomatoes into thin strips; place on top. Sprinkle with 1 teaspoon dried rosemary and kosher salt to taste. Bake until hot; cut into wedges. ● Soup for four: Simmer a 9-ounce package of fresh tortellini in 6 cups chicken broth until cooked. Add 5 chopped dried tomatoes and 1 cup frozen peas; heat. Sprinkle with grated Parmesan.

Canny Containers

CAN #	FLUID OUNCES	CUPS
#1	15.6	2
303, cylinder	19.0	2⅓
#2½	28.5	3½
#5	56.0	7
#10	103.7	12¾
1 gallon	128.0	16

CHAPTER 4

Errand Enhancers

Pick up the dry cleaning. Drop off the dog at the groomer. Carpool the kids to soccer practice. For many of us, car time is an "unavoidable waste" of time. But it doesn't have to be. You can turn those hours behind the wheel into productive time for yourself and your family.

> You can get it all done with less stress and with time to spare. Use maps, make lists, take control!

Plan Ahead

● Make a list of everything you need to do—and check each item off as you go. This way you won't have to backtrack for something you've forgotten.

● Take the time to figure out, geographically, the order of your errands. Look at a map if necessary to determine the most efficient course to follow.

● Group errands together. If you're going to the dry cleaner, check your master list to see what else you can do in that part of town.

● In your car, keep a map of your immediate area. It may sound obvious, but most people consult a map only when they're in unfamiliar territory. However, consulting a map can help you chart your course, look for shortcuts, and in the event of a traffic tie-up or detour, get back on track quickly.

● Whenever you go to the store to buy a staple—milk, eggs, toilet paper—buy two instead of one. When you start to use the second carton of eggs, enter that item on your shopping list. You'll save yourself from going to the store to pick up just one thing.

Spellbound

● Between work, friends, phone calls, and the like, it's difficult to find uninterrupted time to help kids study their spelling words. Why not try this? When you're chauffeuring your kids to and from their activities, instead of listening to the radio, practice their weekly spelling words. They will learn their own words and each other's too. And you've bought yourself some extra "me" time for later.

Size Matters

● Keep a list of your family's clothing sizes in your wallet. When you stumble upon a particularly good buy, you can take advantage of it to save both time and money.

A size list takes the guesswork out of shopping.

Game Plan

● You know what it's like—baseball practice ran long, and that roast you planned to cook will never get done in time for dinner. What to do? Keep coupons for a variety of restaurants and take-out places in the glove compartment of your car. That way, when you know there's no time to make dinner, you can stop to pick something up on the way home or grab a meal at a restaurant with the kids on the way to an activity.

Household Vitals

● If you're currently in the process of redecorating or remodeling your home, fill a small notebook with vital house statistics—room and window sizes, paint colors, wallpaper samples, rug fibers— and stow it in the car or a tote bag. When you're out shopping for furniture or paint, there's no need to go home to see if a piece will fit or the color matches—you'll have your notebook to refer to.

Homeowner's helper: a book filled with sizes, swatches, stains, and more.

● Another good idea: Keep an address book listing the hours and phone numbers of the shops you frequent, including (but not limited to) the beauty salon, dry cleaner, library, butcher, and video store. By knowing the hours, you'll never be late for a drop-off or pickup again.

● Keep a camera in your car and snap pictures of exterior paint colors, architectural elements, and landscape designs you like. When it's time to remodel, you'll have an idea portfolio.

Video Picks

● Does this happen to you? You think about a movie you'd like to rent, but when you get to the video store, you can never remember which movie it was. Try this: Keep a mail-order video catalog in the car's glove compartment and circle the tapes you and your family want to rent when you think of them. The next time you're at the video store, just scan the pages of the catalog for your preselected choices.

Shop but No Time to Stop?

● You can squeeze in grocery shopping between carpool destinations. Just stow a small cooler in the trunk of your car and put perishable groceries—milk, eggs, butter, cheese—in your portable "ice box" so they don't spoil.

Day-to-Night Strategy

● When you can't go home to freshen up for after-work dinner meetings and social gatherings, you can still give yourself a quick pick-me-up. How? Keep a makeup case filled with hair spray, brush and comb, toothpaste and toothbrush, a small bottle of mouthwash, and an atomizer of cologne in the glove compartment or your handbag. No matter where you're going, you'll have what you need to give yourself a beauty lift.

Getting There

● Keep a book with see-through sleeves in your car to compile a "How to Get There" notebook alphabetized by destination. Include concise instructions on which exits and streets to take and the best places to eat, for example. Also note the phone number of the destination so you can call if a problem arises.

You can keep your eyes on the road when you tape-record directions.

Turn right at second signal...

● It's sometimes difficult to read written directions while you're trying to find an unfamiliar destination, especially at night. One solution: Tape-record yourself reading the directions. While you're driving, you can listen to the tape to get where you're going. You don't need to take your eyes from the road, and you can stop or replay the tape as needed.

● Here's a way to put last year's telephone books to good use—keep them in the trunk of your car. When you're out and about and need to find, say, a hardware or auto parts store, you can look through the book to find one that's close to where you are. You'd be surprised how much time and excess running around this can save you.

Shopping Sanity Savers

● Never take a hungry child to the supermarket with you. If for some reason you end up in a grocery store when you know your child is hungry, pick something up from the aisle that he or she can eat while you shop (paying for it, of course, at the checkout on your way out). Make sure you buy something that's not gooey, messy, or too sweet. Crackers, some cereals, and fruit are all good choices for in-store munchies.

● Let your toddler bring his or her own toy grocery cart to the store with you so that you can "shop" together. Your youngster can retrieve items off the lower shelves when appropriate, or you can share small, unbreakable items from your cart.

● Grade-school kids can "add up" your purchases as you go through the aisles. Give them a calculator and let them figure out the bill before you get to the register. It'll be fun for them to see how close they came to the real total and provides a good lesson on the cost of food.

● Your children will feel empowered if you let them make a few of the buying decisions. Allow them to choose the flavor yogurt you buy that week, or pick out the fruits and vegetables they want. You can always work in a nutrition lesson about why something is a good food and why something else isn't.

● Divide your grocery shopping list and give it to the older kids. They can help you find needed items from shelves and even calculate the better buys. (As an incentive, you can let them keep the money they save using coupons and discounts!) You get your shopping done more quickly, and they get valuable "life" training.

● When shopping for clothes for your children, try to take one child at a time and turn your excursion into a "date." To tip the scales in your favor, make sure your son or daughter gets to bed early the night before and eats a hearty, healthy breakfast in the morning. (Remember, a hungry child is a cranky child.) Have specific shopping goals in mind—summer clothes, outfits for school,

Timing Is Everything: 5 Ways to Beat the Rush

● Unless it's an emergency, schedule doctors' appointments early in the morning or just after lunch. See your dentist during lunch hour if possible.

● If you need a home repair or service person, try to schedule the appointment so you're the first one of the day. This way you won't be waiting if he or she happens to get backed up.

● Avoid banks on Fridays; the first, fifteenth, and thirtieth of each month; and any day at lunch hour. Better yet, bank by mail or modem.

● Ask your doctor to phone in your prescription to the pharmacy so you can avoid the 15- to 60-minute wait while it's being filled.

● Never shop for groceries the day before a holiday.

special-occasion clothes—and stay on track, or you'll tire out your youngster without getting what you need. Break for lunch at a restaurant, and end the day at a kid-friendly locale: a park, an arcade, someplace that you can use as incentive to get the utmost cooperation from your youngster while you shop.

Two carts are better than one when youngsters help you shop.

Things to Do While Waiting in Your Car

● Reconcile your checkbook.
● Clean out your purse.
● Touch up your makeup.
● Gather up car debris into one of the plastic trash bags you stow in your glove compartment.
● Sort through your mail.
● Write invitations, thank-you notes, even postcards to friends to keep in touch.
● Rifle through coupons and toss expired ones.
● Make out your grocery shopping list.

Delegate, Delegate

● Teenagers, especially those who have learned to drive, will often jump at the chance to do an errand if it means they get the car. Let them go to the car wash, dry cleaner, dog groomer. It keeps them busy and lightens your load.
● Share the workload by trading off errands and carpool duty with friends. You offer to take the kids to basketball practice on Monday; your friend will pick up bulk staples for you at the wholesale club on Friday.

Kept waiting? Use the time to clean out your purse.

Special Delivery

● Whenever possible, take advantage of delivery service—from your dry cleaner, grocer, or pharmacist. Even if you're charged a small fee, you may find it worthwhile for the time and energy you save.

Phone from Home

● If you're going to the store to pick up a particular item, call ahead first to make sure they have it and can put it aside for you. Doing so can turn your shopping stops into quick ins and outs.

Mail-Order Mania

● If you love to leaf through the catalogs that arrive en masse in your mailbox, why not take advantage of the convenience mail-order shopping offers? You can shop when you want—even in your pajamas—since most catalog toll-free ordering lines are open 24 hours a day, seven days a week. For an added fee, most companies offer overnight delivery (a procrastinator's dream come true).
● Avoid the crowds at malls and on the road (particularly at holiday time), and even have your presents mailed directly to the recipient, sometimes gift-wrapped.
● Merchandise is not the only gift option. If someone on your list loves a particular catalog, send that person a gift certificate from the company.

● If you don't already receive catalogs and want to start getting them, write to Mail Preference Service, c/o Direct Marketing Association, P.O. Box 9008, Farmingdale, NY 11735-9008, and request that your name be added to the direct-mail list.

● If you'd rather not clog up your mailbox with a plethora of paper, check out the mail-order catalogs at your local library. Make a copy of the pages that have your desired items, plus a copy of the order form. If you don't want to receive this or other catalogs, when you place your order you must specify that you do not want your name added to their mailing list.

● Before you order, check out the company's guaranteed-satisfaction and return policies. If you don't like the item once it arrives, you may not be happy with a credit rather than a refund.

● Fill out the order form carefully and make a copy of it if you're mailing it in. (Even if you're ordering by phone, fill out the form completely. It's a good way to have a record of what you ordered.)

● Ask the customer service representative specific questions about the item you're ordering. If it's clothing, for example, ask about the weight of the fabric and the construction. Is the item lined? Does it need dry-cleaning?

● Inquire about freight and shipping charges. Often there is a minimum shipping charge, no matter how small your order is. If you don't want to order much from one catalog, perhaps you can get some friends to add some items to your order and then split the shipping charges.

● Know the return policy of each mail-order catalog before you place an order. You will want to know if there is a time limit on returns (particularly if you're shopping early for Christmas, for example) or if there are restrictions. If you send an item back, follow the company's directions exactly, usually found on the original packing slip. If you have lost this slip, include a letter listing the product, its item number, the reason for return, your credit-card number if applicable, and your name and address with zip code. Then send the merchandise by insured mail, return receipt.

● Never send cash. Use a check, money order, or credit card. Credit-card purchases make returns easier—your account can be credited when merchandise is sent back, and if there is a problem, you can request that the disputed charge be taken off your bill until there is a resolution. Check your monthly statement to make sure the account is adjusted. It may take one or two billing cycles for the credit to appear.

● If you cannot successfully resolve a mail-order dispute, the Direct Marketing Association can help. Send a detailed letter explaining your grievance to Direct Marketing Association, Mail Order Action Line, 1111 19th St. NW, Suite 1100, Washington, DC 20036.

Shopping.calm

● Take advantage of shopping through the Internet. Shop at your convenience from home and browse the Web for whatever you need (see the following list of Nifty Web Sites). If you can't find what you're looking for on our list, log on to ShopGuide.com **(www.shopguide.com).** Additionally, most of the major search engines have links to shopping sites.

Remember, before making any online purchase, verify that the site you're buying from has a secured server to protect your credit-card number and other personal information. If the site is secured, you'll receive a message saying something like "Entering Secure Site." Or, conversely, "Submitting Unsecured Information." If you are unsure about the security of a site, place your order over the phone. Happy surfing!

Toys
Gift Baskets
Food, Wine, Flowers
Movies and Music
Books and Magazines
Electronic Stuff
Hammacher Schlemmer

Cybershopping means you never need to find a parking space.

Shopping on the Internet: 50 Nifty Web Sites

There are new Web sites popping up every day, but these established sites should cover just about everyone on your list.

TOYS

etoys
www.etoys.com
Choose from among hundreds of brand-name toys without fighting crowded aisles to get them. The gift center will even offer ideas for specific age and price ranges. You can have your present wrapped with a personalized card.

GoldenMonkey Toys and Collectibles Shop
www.goldenmonkey.com
If you're looking for the latest trendsetting gift or a one-of-a-kind collectible, this is the site to browse.

Red Rocket
www.redrocket.com
Clueless about what to give your 6-year-old niece and 10-year-old nephew? This site is part store and part service center. It will recommend award-winning, best-selling books and toys from a dozen makers. Choose from one of four designs of gift wrap.

Gund Online
www.gund.com
High-quality stuffed animals for less than retail price.

FAO Schwarz
www.faoschwarz.com
All kinds of toys for all kinds of children—delivered and wrapped in FAO's signature rocking-horse wrapping paper.

SmartKids' Toys
www.smartkidstoys.com
Inventive, educational, and scientific toys. Select from three gift wrappings.

Stuffed Animal World
www.stuffed-animals.com
Not just your run-of-the-mill teddy bears, a menagerie of plush animals can be found on this site.

Wal-Mart Online
www.wal-mart.com
The toy department here excels in perennial favorites, like classic board games, model airplanes, miniature schoolhouses, and train parts.

GIFT BASKETS AND CLOTHES
The Basket Hound
www.baskethound.com
Unique gifts artfully arranged in all kinds of baskets, from $30 to $100.

GiftTree
www.gifttree.com
Most of these baskets feature chocolates, candies, baked goods, and other gourmet treats. You'll also find theme baskets containing wine, pasta, handmade soaps, and cigars. Prices start at $30.

Uptown Baskets
www.giftsforyou.com
Looking for more customized baskets? Uptown sells everything from lobster bakes to potpourri. Prices start at $40.

Clothesnet.com
www.clothesnet.com
Need a new ensemble? Start here. Clothesnet.com links to dozens of designer sites and online retail shops for men, women, and children.

Lands' End
www.landsend.com
You'll find affordable, durable family apparel here, with a strong emphasis on customer service.

Spiegel
www.spiegel.com
Though not as comprehensive as the catalog, this site is extensive and easy to navigate.

The Ultimate Outlet
www.ultimateoutlet.com
From Spiegel's home page, link to The Ultimate Outlet, which offers an array of discounted past-season and overstock items.

The Gap
www.gap.com
Here's a site that offers a hefty dose of style and substance too. The same basic products found in the store can be purchased electronically. Returns can be either mailed back or taken to the nearest retail outlet.

FOOD, WINE, AND FLOWERS

Dean & Deluca
www.dean-deluca.com
The famous gourmet store's mouth-watering festival of food is now available digitally. Most orders are shipped overnight express.

Ethel M Chocolates
www.ethelm.com
Named for the mother of Frank Mars of candy bar fame, Ethel M offers deluxe boxed chocolates. Choose from many prepackaged gift boxes or create your own.

Fran's Chocolates, Ltd.
www.franschocolates.com
Elegant chocolates elegantly packaged.

Jelly Belly
www.jellybelly.com
Gift assortments, tins, and jars filled with jelly beans in 40 true-to-life flavors.

The Garlic Store
www.thegarlicstore.com
For the gourmet cook and gourmand alike, you can order deluxe heads of "the stinking rose," as well as sauces, snacks, cookbooks, and kitchenware.

Grafton Village Cheese Company
www.graftonvillagecheese.com
A wide array of regular and flavored Cheddar cheeses, along with Vermont maple syrup and corncob-smoked hams and bacon.

Harry and David
www.harryanddavid.com
Luscious fruits, baked goods, nuts, and dried fruits elegantly packaged.

OmahaSteaks.com
www.omahasteaks.com
This mail-order purveyor of top-quality cuts of beef now offers the same service via the Web. Ordering is easy, and there's a 100-percent-satisfaction guarantee. Within a week your steaks will arrive packed with dry ice in a reusable cooler.

Peets Coffee & Tea
www.peets.com
A well-known San Francisco Bay area coffee emporium now sells a wide array of coffee and tea blends on the Internet.

wine.com
aol.wine.com
Extensive wine lists, including a large "Bang for the Buck" category, as well as expert advice make this a great wine "shop."

Phillip's 1-800-Florals
www.800florals.com
FTD.com
www.ftd.com
1-800-flowers.com
www.1800flowers.com
While selections and prices at each of these three sites are similar, service separates them. Phillip's offers same-day service for orders in by noon, FTD by 1 P.M., and 1-800-Flowers by 2 P.M.

MOVIES AND MUSIC

CDNOW
www.cdnow.com
This site offers a large selection and expanded search features.

CD Universe
www.cduniverse.com
If you do a lot of online shopping, you'll appreciate this site's efficient and speedy interface.

Mass Music
www.massmusic.com
A great resource for hard-to-find imports. This site also offers music accessories, including CD racks and tape cleaners.

Tunes.com
www.tunes.com
This site offers the best and widest selection of "streaming audio" song clips—a direct broadcast of music to your computer.

Reel.com
www.reel.com
In addition to sales, this site offers online film classes with lectures by cinematic experts.

Yahoo! Music Shopping
http://shopping.yahoo.com/music
This is a good site to visit if you know exactly what you're shopping for. When you enter the name of the record, you'll see an up-to-the-second list of the going rates from a couple dozen or so major sites.

shop.film.com
http://film.bige.com
At this premier shopping site for movies, you can search by title, actor, or director. The site sells new and used videos, DVDs, laser discs, soundtracks, books, memorabilia— you name it. Selection is vast, and prices are good too.

Home Vision Cinema
www.homevision.com
For those with specialized taste in film, including collectors of restored and rare, hard-to-find films, Home Vision Cinema is the source.

BOOKS AND MAGAZINE SUBSCRIPTIONS

Amazon.com
www.amazon.com
You can find just about any title published in the last 20 years, plus author interviews, reviews, synopses, and more. Gifts are shipped, wrapped with a personalized card if you like, with speed and nice extra touches, like a bookmark.

Barnes & Noble
www.barnesandnoble.com
The selection isn't as large as Amazon's, but the discounts are sometimes greater. The site offers very good descriptions of magazine titles.

Bibliofind
www.bibliofind.com
Use this site to hunt down out-of-print and hard-to-find books.

Books.com
www.books.com
Though it doesn't have as extensive a selection as either Amazon or Barnes & Noble, this site does offer deep discounts and has a large "Independent Press" section that highlights small publishers.

Books For Cooks
www.books-for-cooks.com
Cookbook lovers rejoice! This Internet store offers over 10,000 titles organized into 140 shopping categories.

MysteryNet Books
www.mysterynet.com/books
If whodunits are your thing or you yearn for "mysterious" news, check out this site, which places orders through Amazon's site.

ALLMAGS MAGAZINE SHOP
http://allmags.hypermart.net
You'll find subscriptions to more than 800 magazines at savings of up to 85% off retail prices.

ELECTRONICS
Value America
www.valueamerica.com
This popular site sells more than just home electronics; its lineup includes toys, games, and PCs. The prices are competitive, especially if you are a member (it's free) and information about store policies is clearly written and easy to find.

AudioVideo.com
www.audiovideo.com
A great assortment of electronic equipment can be found here, often at prices generally lower than you'll find at discount stores.

Crutchfield
www.crutchfield.com
This easy-to-use site lets you search by category, brand, or model number and the selection is impressive. The pricing is competitive and shipping on returned goods is free.

CompareNet
www.compare.net
This huge and useful site helps you make product choices by giving you detailed product information, reviews, and even side-by-side charts. Techno jargon also gets explained away, and you can often buy the products you want through linked sites.

hifi.com
www.hifi.com
This New England–based chain offers direct online sales and excellent factory-direct deals.

Hammacher Schlemmer
www.hammacher.com
If getting the best in electronic gear is your goal and price isn't an issue, check out this Web site. The company has been offering unique and unusual products since 1848.

An End to Morning Madness

The way your morning begins often sets the tone for the rest of the day. And for many of us, that tone is frantic. With only a small window—two hours at best—to get everyone ready for work, school, day care, it's no wonder we start our day with that "already-behind-the-eight-ball" kind of feeling. But there are things you can do to give everyone a less hectic send-off. By following these tried-and-true tips, you'll even have time to read the paper over a leisurely cup of coffee before you leave.

Rush hour—and you haven't left the house? We'll tell you how to stop the clock.

Seize the Day

● Wake up an hour before everyone else in your house. That way you get the jump on the day and not the other way around. Exercise, have your coffee, shower, and put on your makeup. What you miss in sleep time, you make up in having a less frenzied first hour of the morning to yourself.

Easing Bathroom Bottlenecks

If the first "traffic jam" you encounter in the morning is in the bathroom, you need to set up some congestion-preventing rules:

● Children age 10 and under bathe or shower the night before; 11 and older shower in the morning.

● The oldest child should get up 15 minutes earlier than the next older child, and so on. Older kids usually spend more time getting ready in the morning.

● Moms and dads get first dibs on the bathroom because they usually have to oversee the younger children.

● Share the bathroom. While one person showers, another person can be brushing teeth, drying hair, or putting on makeup.

● Place an inexpensive kitchen timer in the bathroom. Use it to limit bathroom time to 15 minutes a person. Make a game of playing "beat the clock" with your younger children. Award the youngster who beat the clock most often first (or last) dibs on the bathroom the following week.

● Allow older siblings to help younger ones prep for school. They can braid hair and tie shoes to help make your morning less hectic.

Alarming Ideas

● To facilitate the staggered wake-up calls, make sure everyone in your family has an alarm clock. It will motivate each child to be responsible for his or her own schedule and give you more time in the morning.

● For those hard-to-roust members of your family, relocate their alarm clock to a distant part of their room so they have to get out of bed to turn it off.

Get up an hour earlier and reclaim some quality time for yourself.

Chart a New Course

● Sometimes a visual reminder—especially when you're trying to establish a new routine—can keep things moving along. Create a chart of all the tasks your child must accomplish in the morning. Set it up so it's sequential—brush teeth, get dressed, comb hair, and eat breakfast, for example—and let your youngster check off each task after he or she has completed it.

● Use positive reinforcement—praise, a prize at the end of the week, extra bathroom time, whatever works for each child—to encourage everyone to keep up the momentum.

Before-School Rules

● Pack lunches (keep refrigerated) and backpacks or folders the night before.
● Everyone should be dressed and ready to go before breakfast.
● Make—and enforce—a no-television-before-school rule. The fewer the distractions, the greater the likelihood your youngster will get out of the house on time.
● Discourage before-school phone calls—both placing and receiving them—except when truly necessary. This helps to keep you and your kids on schedule and, by eliminating unnecessary disruptions, maintains a semblance of much-needed calm in the early morning rush hour.

Preparation Station

Visual reminders, such as charts, keep everybody on track in the A.M.

● Pick a spot—usually by the door—to put fully loaded backpacks, coats, hats, briefcases, and weather-specific footwear. This alleviates the scramble to get everything together when the bus or carpool arrives.
● Hang several hooks by the back door for keys. Have everyone get in the habit of automatically hanging keys on these hooks whenever they enter the house. Not having to search for keys in the morning is an incredible time-saver.

Fill It Up

● Gas up cars on the way home from work or school, not on the way to your destination. You usually have fewer time constraints on your way home, and you won't get frustrated if you have to wait behind a car or two to fill up.

Make all carpool arrangements the night before. Don't wait until morning to find out how each child will be getting to soccer practice, scout meeting, or dance class.

Whenever possible and practical, pack the car the night before, especially if you have several stops to make in the morning. This not only saves time but also lessens the chances of forgetting something vital.

Kids' backpacks tend to look very similar, as do diaper bags for toddlers at day care. To set yours apart from the rest, attach a picture-frame key chain with your child's photo in it to the bag. You'll never mix up whose bag belongs to whom, either on the way out of the house or when you're picking your child up.

Breakfast Treats

Put out bowls of cereal the night before and cover them with plastic wrap or a lid. In the morning the older children can help younger ones pour the milk on. This frees you from having to oversee breakfast so that you can concentrate on other things.

Keep some breakfast-worthy foods—breakfast bars, juice boxes—in the car. They'll come in super handy on those mornings when you just can't find time for a meal in the house.

Always have hard-boiled eggs or a bowl of fresh whole fruit at the ready on a convenient shelf in the refrigerator. That way there's always something "grabbable" for breakfast as you or your youngsters dash out the door.

If you make waffles, pancakes, or French toast on the weekends, always make an extra batch or two to freeze. Pack single-size servings in resealable plastic bags. These heat up quickly in the microwave or toaster—and everyone enjoys them.

Think "drinks" when it comes to breakfast. Use a blender to make a delicious and nutritious breakfast drink: Combine plain nonfat yogurt with your fruit of choice (peaches, strawberries, bananas, or any flavorful combination), a sweetener, such as honey or brown sugar, skim milk, and ice cubes. Blend the mixture until thick and frothy.

The 5-Minute Face

EYES	FACE	CHEEKS	LIPS
1 minute: Stroke on brown or taupe shadow along the crease; blend. **30 seconds:** Coat upper lashes with one layer of mascara.	**1 minute:** Apply foundation with a sponge. **30 seconds:** Dust cheeks, forehead, nose, and chin lightly with pressed powder.	**30 seconds:** Sweep soft peach blush across the apples of cheeks for healthy-looking color. This color works well for all skin types.	**1 minute:** Line lips and apply lipstick with a lip brush. A brush is versatile and allows for more precision. Blot.

● Keep a stash of disposable drink cups with lids and straws on hand so that you or your kids can take the "portable potable" with you.

● Every once in a while, go out for breakfast. This is an especially wonderful treat for yourself during overly hectic times—during the holidays, for example. There's nothing like being served to reduce the pace a notch or two for the rest of the day.

Lunch Bunch

● To ease the morning "rush hours" before school, let kids help make their lunches the night before. Not only does this give you extra time in the morning, but it eliminates complaints from the kids about what's in their lunch boxes.

● As an inducement to encourage kids to make their own lunches, try this: Tell them for each lunch they prepare instead of purchase, they get to keep the lunch money for themselves. You'll be surprised how eager they'll be to brown-bag it.

● Keep a jar of change in the kitchen or dining room so you and the kids can grab lunch or transportation money on the way out of the house.

● Prepare two or three days' worth of lunch sandwiches (without condiments) in one evening and freeze them. As they thaw in the lunch box or bag, the bread becomes soft and fresh tasting.

● Collect condiment packets— mayonnaise, ketchup, mustard— from fast-food and take-out restaurants and keep them in a bowl near the refrigerator. When you pack those frozen sandwiches, toss the desired condiment packet in the lunch bag; add to the sandwich at lunchtime.

Hurry-Up Beauty

● No time to set your hair in the morning? To give your do a quick lift, mist your hairbrush with hair spray and lightly run it through your hair. This method also works well on flattened "hat hair."

● For a fast way to curl long hair, sweep your hair into a high ponytail and roll the "tail" with two or three hot rollers or use a large-diameter curling iron. Allow the rollers to cool, then unroll the ponytail and remove it from its holder for a full head of curls.

● If you're a little "sleepy-eyed" in the morning, here's a way to revitalize those tired eyes: Use a bisque-colored shadow over the entire lid to open up the eye area and give you a bright-eyed look.

Mist your brush with hair spray to give limp locks a lift.

● Don't use eyeliner on tired eyes—it only accentuates the bagginess.

● Forget mascara when you're in a rush. Just use an eyelash curler. Your lashes will look longer and lusher.

● Keep a small jar of petroleum jelly in your makeup bag. A small dab on lips and lashes makes them look made up without cosmetics. Perfect for days when a casual look is all you need or for times when you know you'll be redoing your makeup later for an evening out.

Best Face Forward

● To cut down on the amount of time it takes to put on your makeup in the morning, mix your own, using equal parts base and moisturizer. The makeup mix glides easily onto your skin, and it's the perfect canvas for blush and powder. Another plus: Your makeup will come off just as easily.

Quick Fix for Nails

● Why spend money on those quick-drying nail sprays, oils, and polishes? To dry newly applied nail polish, just dip your fingertips in a glass of ice water.

Clothes Encounters

The key to successful dressing is planning, preparation, and paring your routine down to basics. Here's how:

Nail polish sets faster after fingertips take an "ice bath."

● Children should choose their outfits the night before school and lay or hang them somewhere that's convenient in the room.

● Dress very young children— toddlers and babies—before they're out of the crib and fully awake. They won't fuss as much.

● When you put your kids' clothes on hangers or in drawers, hang or fold them together as outfits—with socks, barrettes, belts, and other accessories tucked in a pocket. This way, when the kids choose an outfit, they'll have everything they need to look great.

● Try to keep a separate color scheme in mind for each child when you purchase school clothing: blue for your older boy, red for your younger boy, purple for your girl. This makes getting dressed in the morning easier. Any of the tops and bottoms will work with each other because they are in the same color family.

WEEKLY WINNERS

● Wash out a week's worth of panty hose on the weekends. This way you're sure to have a pair a day at the ready for those busy workday mornings.

● Tuck a fresh handkerchief in the pocket of each of your spouse's work shirts, and he'll always have one handy.

● When your dresses and suits come back from the dry cleaner, accessorize them before you put them away. Put pins on lapels; tie scarves around the hanger; tuck costume jewelry in the pockets. When you're pressed for time in the morning, you'll appreciate having all the extras already in place.

SHOE CHIC

● If you wear sneakers or walking shoes to work and tote a pair of shoes to change into, why not leave a pair or two of shoes at the office? You won't have to worry about packing them up before you leave for work in the morning, and you'll free up some room in your closet at home.

● If your shoes need a quick shine before you're out the door, dab some furniture polish on a soft cloth and wipe it on the shoes. The polish cleans and shines at the same time.

CLING FREE

● Static cling giving you that "creeping" feeling? Squirt a small amount of moisturizer on the palms of your hands and then rub your hands over your panty hose underneath your dress or skirt. Presto! No more cling.

> **A little dab of lotion is all you need to keep clothes from creeping up.**

● For another terrific static cling fighter, try used dryer fabric-softener sheets. Tuck a few in your purse and use them whenever clothes start to creep up on you. Rub them over your panty hose or socks, under slacks, or on linings or slips.

● Garments cut on the bias don't ride up. If you sew, make your own bias-cut slips—you'll save money and never worry about creeping layers.

WORRY NOT

● Keep several sewing needles threaded and handy—tucked in a makeup case or change purse—for fashion emergencies like a popped button or undone hem. Use basic thread colors: black, white, brown, and navy.

● Another container for sewing needles and threads: an empty dental-floss case. Wind some thread around the spool where the dental floss used to be, then add some sewing needles, small buttons, and safety pins. Make up a few of these fix-it kits to tuck into every purse you have. No matter where you go or what you're wearing, you'll be ready for a clothing emergency.

● Keep a lint brush in the glove compartment of your car or in your briefcase. That way you're always ready for a quick lint pickup, wherever you are.

● Another must-have wardrobe remedy: clear nail polish. Not only can you use it to stop an errant run in your panty hose, but you can also dab a drop or two on loose or weak button threads to shore them up.

● Use clear nail polish on the ends of older sneaker laces when the plastic coating has worn off. This makes it easy again to lace up sneakers.

10 Great Rush-Hour Breakfasts

That morning meal is too important to skimp on, especially since so many of us shortchange ourselves at other meals. These tasty and tempting dishes can be prepared in 15 minutes or less.

1. VITAMIN C SMOOTHIE

Place 1 cup frozen vanilla yogurt and 1 cup fresh orange juice in a blender; whirl to combine. Add 1 mango and 1 papaya, both pitted, peeled, and chopped, and 2 cups hulled strawberries. Whirl until smooth.

2. YOGURT CONE

Fill an ice cream cone with layers of vanilla yogurt and small pieces of soft fruit, such as bananas, peaches, or strawberries. Top with granola.

3. OATMEAL BAKED APPLE

Core a large apple and microwave on high for 2 minutes. Fill the center of the apple with instant oatmeal, add water, and pop back in the microwave for another 2 or 3 minutes, until the oatmeal is cooked. Top with raisins and brown sugar. The perfect breakfast for a cold winter morning.

4. JAM SANDWICH

Heat precooked pancakes, French toast slices, or waffles in a microwave or toaster oven. Spread one pancake, waffle, or slice of French toast with all-fruit jam, jelly, or preserves. Top with a second one to make a take-along sandwich.

5. APPLESAUCE ANNIE

Add a scoop of cottage cheese to an individual cup of naturally sweetened chunky applesauce. Sprinkle with bran cereal for a little crunch.

6. BREAKFAST WRAP

Here's an all-in-one breakfast for four that can go out the door with you. Heat a nonstick skillet coated with nonstick cooking spray. Brown 2 ounces diced Canadian bacon. Beat 4 eggs with ¼ cup reduced-fat sour cream and 2 teaspoons chopped fresh chives. Add to the skillet. Cook until the eggs are set—for about 5 minutes. Remove from the heat. Heat 4 tortillas according to package directions. Spoon one-fourth of the egg mixture into the center of each tortilla. Fold the bottom end up, then wrap the sides.

7. EGG SALAD PITA

To 1 chopped hard-boiled egg, add a scoop of cottage cheese, chopped onion or chives, and salt and pepper to taste. Mix and stuff into a pita.

8. MUFFIN MELT

Toast an English muffin. In a nonstick skillet coated with nonstick cooking spray, brown a slice of Canadian bacon. Place the bacon slice, a tomato slice, and 1 slice of Swiss or American cheese on one half of the muffin. Microwave on medium for 30 seconds or until the cheese just starts to melt. Top with the other muffin half.

9. BAGEL SPREADS

Mix jarred baby food fruit—the chunky kind—into cottage cheese or yogurt that's been drained of its liquid. Spread this on a toasted bagel. More nutritious than cream cheese or butter.

10. PEANUT BUTTER TOAST

Spread one side of toasted multi-grain bread with peanut butter. Top with fruit spread, raisins, or wheat germ.

Kid Pleasin' Pastimes

"There's no one to play with." "I'm bored." "I have nothing to do." The strains of these whiny refrains are enough to send any parent over the edge. The hints we've assembled in this chapter will make you a wiz at thinking up fun stuff for kids to do. (We won't tell them where you got the ideas!) Best of all, most of these games, crafts, and activities use materials and other things you probably already have in your house. So let the games begin!

With our kid-friendly activities, there's always something fun to do.

Learn and Earn

● Here's a way to encourage your older youngster to read. Pay your "big kid" 10 cents for every book he or she reads to a younger sibling. Everyone benefits from the reading hour, including you.

Write Away

● To give kids some letter-writing motivation—and practice—treat each one to a box of personalized stationery every year. They can use it to write letters to their grandparents, cousins, and friends.

● Another way to encourage kids to put pen to paper is to have them write letters: requests for free samples from companies that offer them, notes to various chambers of commerce for information about cities they'd like to visit, letters of praise for products or services they liked, complaint letters for things that they didn't, even fan letters. It's a good life lesson, and your kids will eagerly retrieve mail for you in the hopes that a letter has arrived for them.

Young Artists at Play

● When using tempera paint with your children, squeeze a little bit of each color around the outer edge of a large paper plate. They can use the center of the plate for mixing the colors and simply toss the plate in the trash when they're through.

● A Styrofoam egg carton makes an excellent—and free—paint palette. Just squeeze some paint into each of the egg cups. Leave a few empty for those "custom colors" your young artist creates. When the art project is finished, toss the carton in the garbage.

● Plastic syrup bottles—the kind with the pull-up top—make excellent squirt guns. In the summer, let the kids fill them with water and hose each other down.

● If you have a snowy winter, refill the empty plastic syrup bottles with water and food coloring. Kids will have a ball "painting" the snow different colors.

Toys for Sale!

● Let your kids have a garage sale of their own. A garage sale is a terrific learning opportunity for kids (and not a bad way to eliminate some playroom clutter). Chances are they have many toys that they've outgrown, are broken, or are missing pieces. Ask your kids to clean out their toy boxes, the basement,

An empty egg carton is just the thing for a young artist's paints.

and the garage and tell them that whatever money they earn, they can keep to buy something special. This isn't a one-day project—it will probably take your children the better part of a week or more to pull it all together. And there's enough activity to allow all of your children (and even their friends) in on the act. They can:

Make signs to post around the neighborhood.

Price each item with a price sticker.

Organize toys into groups.

Handle money and make change. This depends upon the age of your children; generally, a child seven or older will be up to the task.

Sell lemonade or iced tea to thirsty shoppers.

Coin Countdown

● If you've got a large jar of coins, let your kids count and roll those pennies, nickels, dimes, and quarters. Use the money for a family outing, such as an afternoon at the movies, bowling, roller skating, or horseback riding.

Watch It Grow

● Have your kids cut off the tops of carrots and place them in a shallow tray of water. When roots form, they can plant them in soil.

● Show children how to stick toothpicks into an avocado pit and suspend it so it sits halfway into a jar of water. Very soon they will see an avocado tree spring from the pit.

● Don't toss those orange, lemon, or grapefruit seeds. Let your kids plant them ½ inch deep in peat moss in a sunny spot and keep them moist. Soon the kids will see a small orchard start to form.

A sunflower tepee is the perfect hideaway for little ones.

● You and your children can grow a sunflower tepee. Plant sunflower seeds in a circle wide enough for two children to sit inside. Stick long wooden dowels or bamboo rods in the ground next to the sunflower seeds to create a support structure. Loosely tie the sticks or poles together at the top. As the sunflowers grow, gently tie them to the supports with old panty hose. When the sunflowers are fully grown, your kids can sit inside their homegrown tepee.

● After the sunflowers are grown, have the kids gather some seeds and soak them in water for at least an hour. Then they can string the seeds with an embroidery needle threaded with dental floss to make a sunflower seed necklace. The necklace needs to dry before wearing.

Designing Children

● Let your kids create fancy designs on old T-shirts, sweatshirts, and sneakers with fabric and puff paint. It's a fun project for the kids and gives new life to old clothes.

Beach Blanket Checkers

● Turn an old beach towel into a game board. Here's how: With an indelible marker, draw an 8-inch square on the towel (make sure you have a piece of cardboard underneath the towel so the marker doesn't bleed through to the work surface). With a ruler, divide the square into an 8 x 8 grid (64 boxes total). Color in every other box to create the checkerboard. Make the checkers out of old bottle caps; you'll need at least 15 for each player. Paint each player's checkers a bright color. Sew a pocket on one side of the towel, and use hook-and-loop dots as

This terry-cloth game table is perfect to tote to the beach or park.

fasteners to close the pocket securely. Put the bottle caps in the pocket, roll up the towel, and take it with you to the beach or park.

A Bug's Life

● Empty plastic peanut butter jars make terrific bug catchers. Punch some holes in the lid and let your kids go out to collect "samples." Lightning bugs are particularly fun for young ones to catch, especially at night. Take out a book about bugs from the library so your children can identify their finds.

Scavenger Hunts

● Make up a list of things that can be found outside. You may even want to include some items that come from a place you plan to visit, like a beach or park. Have your kids try to "hunt down" the items on the list. Simplify your list for younger children; expand the search territory to the neighborhood for older ones.

Recycle Pile

Let children turn favorite clothes they can't wear into new things they can use:

● A favorite T-shirt can be stuffed with fiberfill or other soft filling and sewn closed at the neck, bottom, and sleeves to make a comfy, familiar pillow.

● Denim jeans too small? Split the inseams and use a pretty fabric filler wedge to turn the jeans into a skirt.

● Old jeans can also be turned into a sturdy duffel bag or purse. Split open the inseams and then sew the front inseams together and the back inseams together. Cut the bottom to the desired depth of the bag. Use excess denim fabric to make straps or a handle.

● Let your little girl sew the bottom of one of her old dresses closed. Suspend the dress from a hanger, and it becomes a pretty—and personal— pajama bag. Boys can do the same with a large shirt.

● Renew old-looking tennis shoes by sewing or gluing on sequins, lace, patches, or buttons. Or let kids paint on flowers, flames, lightning bolts, animals, or sports logos. Super cool!

Carve Out Some Fun

For children old enough to use a pen knife, these crafts cut the mustard:

● Have them cut a potato in half and carve a design into the cut surface. Then they can press it onto an ink pad and stamp onto paper, cards, or T-shirts.

● Plain old soap can be turned into fun shapes. Let kids pick a design and carefully whittle away at a bar of soap until it takes shape.

Color Fun

● Gather pieces of crayon, peel off any paper that may still be covering them, and put several different colors into one cup of a 12-cup muffin tin. Fill as many cups as you have crayon pieces, making sure to mix the colors. Then place the muffin tin in a 400-degree oven for 10 minutes, or until the crayons melt. Allow the tin to cool completely on a metal rack. When it can be touched, invert it and pop out "crazy crayons." Now when kids color or draw, they'll always be surprised to see the different colors show up. These make great party favors too!

Draw a Crowd

A large roll of brown kraft paper goes a long way toward keeping kids happy:

● Cut out kid-size lengths of paper and have them lie down on the paper and take turns tracing around each other. Then let them draw in their clothes, hair, and faces.

● Use paper to create a mural or backdrop. Pick a destination, like Paris or Italy, and let children paint or draw in the scenery. Afterwards, they can use the backdrop for a play.

● Tack up paper between two walls and let children stand or kneel behind it. Cut out holes where their faces will show through, then let them draw a silly person or group of people around the face holes. They'll have a ball taking turns pretending to be the different characters and putting on "plays" for one another. They'll get a kick out of you taking a turn as well.

Chalk It Up

● Turn your children into "sidewalk" artists by letting them draw on your driveway or sidewalk to their heart's content with different color chalk. It washes away with the rain, but until then they've got a large canvas to create their masterpieces.

● Remember hopscotch? Your children probably don't even know the game. Why not introduce them to it by drawing a board on your driveway and showing them the finer points of hopping, skipping, and jumping over the board. You can even paint a hopscotch board on the floor of your garage or basement for indoor play on bad-weather days.

● Another fun—and easy—outdoor game to make and play: shuffleboard. Show kids how to draw the two large triangles directly across from each other with about 10 feet of open space between them. Divide the triangles into boxes, assigning point values inside each box. Use a peanut butter jar lid for the puck and a broom for the stick, and let them shuffle away.

Chalk turns an ordinary driveway or sidewalk into a game room.

Tykes on Trikes

● Draw a roadway on your driveway, including an intersection and a roundabout, and let little ones on tricycles play "traffic." Children can also take turns being the traffic cop and directing the "drivers."

● For a different twist on the classic children's game "Red Light, Green Light," kids on bikes line up at one end of the driveway, and one child stands at the other end with her back to the cyclers. The child standing alone calls out, "Red light, green light, 1-2-3," still turned away from the kids on trikes. They then try to pedal up to her before she finishes her line and turns around quickly to catch the bikes in motion and send them back to the starting line.

Cardboard Capers

Remember how much fun an empty cardboard appliance box can be? Go to any appliance store or warehouse and ask if they can spare a box or two. (We're sure they'll be thrilled to get rid of them.) Bring them home and let

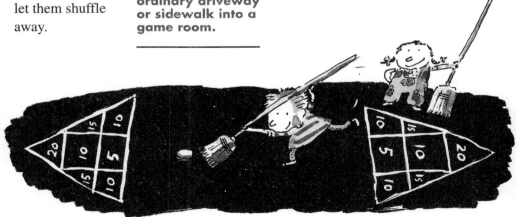

your kids' imaginations run wild. Here are some projects you can do with younger children:

● Paint the outside, cut out windows and a door, and a large box becomes a clubhouse.

● Stand a refrigerator box upright and turn it into a rocket ship. Fold oak tag into a cone to make the capsule on top. Paint the interior of the spaceship black, then affix glow-in-the-dark stars and planets inside. Let kids boldly go where no youngster has ever gone before. . . .

● Turn smaller boxes into "box cars." Remove the top and bottom flaps. Paint the sides to resemble a car, and affix tin-can headlights to the front and red plastic lids for taillights to the back. Knot two lengths of rope from front to back on either side to make shoulder straps so that youngsters can wear their cars. Watch them race around the yard.

Christmas in July

● Decorate an outdoor tree with homemade ornaments from summer finds, like shells, driftwood, and seed pods; string popcorn and cranberries for a garland; top the tree with a tin-foil star; then play Christmas music for kids to sing along to. Make and eat snow cones outside. It's fun to turn the seasons upside down.

See You in September

● To quell those end-of-summer blues, why not throw a back-to-school party? You can have the kids play games— "Pin the Tail on the Donkey," for example—and reward the winners with inexpensive prizes like rulers, crayons, writing paper, pens, pencils, and glue.

Beach Chimes

● Seaside chimes are easy to string together: Snip ten 12-inch lengths of string. Thread shells with holes in them onto six strings and tie small pieces of driftwood to four. Affix the string ends to a piece of driftwood. Hang them all from a branch or porch beam.

Totally Egg-cellent

● Paint a face on a clean eggshell half (be sure to use the round end for the chin). Fill with soil and plant with grass seed. In a few days your egg face will sprout a full head of hair.

Homemade Puzzles

● Paste a photo from a magazine to cardboard, then outline puzzle pieces on the back of the cardboard. Cut them out and you have a custom puzzle. You can do this with photographs too. Enlarge them on a color copier before pasting onto the cardboard, if you wish.

● Write a note on the back of the cardboard before cutting it into puzzle pieces, then send the pieces to a friend. The recipient can read your letter only after putting the puzzle together!

Big Bubble Fun

● Add ¼ cup dishwashing liquid to 4 cups water. Twist wire hangers or floral wire into interesting shapes— stars, hearts, crescent moons—for bubble makers.

10 Rainy Day Activities

These fun activities will keep spirits sunny on even the gloomiest day:

Banish the bad-weather blues with these fun indoor activities.

1. PUPPET THEATER

Let the kids turn those odd socks into hand puppets. They'll need some yarn, glue, buttons, colored markers, fabric remnants, indelible markers, and paint. Then set the stage: Insert a spring-loaded curtain rod in a doorway. If you have an old pair of curtains, hang them from the rod first, or drape fabric over the rod. Puppets appear over the top of the curtain; puppeteers hide behind it.

2. BALLOON SPORTS

A few round latex balloons are all you need to make a day indoors seem like a day at the park. Play balloon basketball by using a wastebasket as the hoop. Or tie some string across two chairs to play balloon volleyball.

3. HOUSE OF CARDS

Let your kids construct a card tower from playing cards. Let them take turns adding to the rows.

4. THE MEMORY GAME

Collect 20 small objects and lay them on a tray or table. Let kids spend 3 minutes trying to memorize what's there. Cover the objects and see who can remember the most. Use fewer objects for smaller children and gradually work up to 20.

● A variation on this game: Put the objects into a paper bag and have players reach in and identify as many as they can by touch.

5. COSTUME BALL

Pull out old costumes and let kids play dress-up. Have them make up a play, creating characters as suggested by the costumes.

6. BOWLED OVER

Collect enough 2-liter soda bottles to use as pins for an indoor bowling game. A tennis or other small, soft ball is just right for indoors.

7. PICNIC INDOORS

Throw a blanket down in the living or family room. Pack a picnic basket complete with sandwiches, hard-boiled eggs, potato chips, cookies, juice boxes, and paper goods. Enjoy your lunch and then tell "campfire" stories to each other when you're done eating.

8. MAKE A "ME" BOOK

With old photos, magazines, cards, and other clippable art, let each of your kids create a scrapbook that's an autobiography. Encourage them to include their own artwork, letters, or anything else that tells their story.

9. LIGHTS, CAMERA, ACTION!

Do you have a video camera at home? Let your kids make a movie of themselves. They can dress up, make up parts, perform different acts, whatever they can think up. Later serve popcorn and soda and invite family and friends over for a screening of the film.

10. TUNE IN

Tell your kids about the golden days of radio, when families gathered round the RCA Victor to listen to the latest tales of *The Shadow* and *The Lone Ranger* or the antics of *Abbott and Costello.* Then show your kids how to make their own own radio show. Just give them a tape recorder, some ideas about sound effects (a flushing toilet, for example, sounds like a bomb going off!), and let them do the rest.

Can Cans: 5 Fun Things to Make with Recycled Tin Cans

Clean empty cans thoroughly and check for sharp edges before you turn them over to the kids.

1. STRIKE UP A TIN-CAN BAND

To begin, collect cans of all sizes. You'll also need some construction or adhesive-backed paper, remnant vinyl, and heavy-duty rubber bands. First, let the children cover the outside of the cans with the paper. Then assemble the band: Use larger cans to make drums by stretching vinyl tightly over the top and securing with rubber bands. Chopsticks make fine drumsticks. To create different-sounding drums,

Kids will love "canned" music.

partially fill the cans with sand. Experiment to get the sound you want.

● To make a string base, you'll need a very large, restaurant-size can. Punch a hole in the center of the bottom and thread a long length of clothesline cord through it (measure it to reach from the floor to your child's shoulder). Knot the cord on the inside of the can. Tie a long stick to the other end of the cord. Place the can, bottom side up, on the ground and rest the stick end not connected to the cord on the top of the can. Kids play this base by placing one foot on the can to hold it down and holding the stick with the tightly strung cord in one hand as they "strum" the cord with the other. Variations of sound are achieved by moving the holding hand up and down the string the way a guitar player changes chords. Shifting the position of the stick also alters the sound. Kids will have a blast with this "instrument." Round out the band with a comb-and-wax-paper kazoo.

● Make maracas out of small cans by fitting a small dowel through a hole punched in the bottom of the can, filling the can with pebbles or dried beans, and covering it tightly with vinyl secured around the top with a heavy-duty rubber band.

2. SILLY STILTS

Punch two holes in the bottom of a large, empty can. Thread a long string (about as long as your child is tall) through the holes, knotting each end on the inside. Repeat with a second can. Turn the cans bottom-up and have your child stand on them, placing each foot through a loop and pulling the loops taut. It's fun to walk on these silly stilts.

3. FUN PHONES

Clean two juice-size tin cans and punch a hole in the center of the bottom of each one. String a long, thin cord through each can with bottoms facing each other. Knot the cord on the inside of the cans. Now your child and a friend can talk privately on their own "phones."

4. CATCH AS CATCH CAN

In the bottom of a medium-size can, punch a hole just large enough to squeeze a few inches of a 12-inch wooden dowel through it. Tie a 12-inch string to the dowel just below the bottom of the can. Tie a large, round wooden bead (the kind with a pre-drilled hole through it) to the other end of the cord. Now you have a homemade cup-and-ball game. The dowel serves as the handle. Your youngster has to swing the cord up to catch the wooden bead in the can.

5. LOONEY LUMINARIAS

Fill a can with water and freeze it. When the water is solid, let your child (over age eight) punch a funny face design into the sides of the can using an awl and hammer. (The ice helps the can keep its shape.) Younger children can draw their design on the can with an indelible marker, and you can punch it out for them. After the ice melts, paint the cans. To light, fill the bottom of the can with sand, place a votive candle inside, and light it for little ones. (Of course, children must be supervised when using luminarias.) This is great for camp-outs.

Phone Diversions

It never fails. You're on the phone, and that's when your kids demand your attention. Here are a few telephone tactics to help you get through at least one call:

● Set a kitchen timer for the amount of time you need to be on the phone, and hand the timer to your youngster. Tell him or her to come get you when the timer goes off.

● Let your little one clip coupons for you while you make phone calls. Keep the store circulars and advertisements from the Sunday paper in a basket by the phone with a pair of safety scissors and, if you have one, your coupon holder. Little children will like having the responsibility of a "grown-up" job; older kids can file coupons by product and weed through your files for expired coupons. Everyone benefits from this arrangement.

● Keep a box or bag full of age-appropriate toys hidden somewhere near the telephone. When your young tyke tries to get your attention as you talk, pull out the phone-only toys. Change the toys frequently to keep little ones interested.

CHAPTER 7

Spending and Saving Made Simple

> If you watch the pennies and nickels, dollars will follow.

A rebate here, a coupon redeemed there, some monetary sleight of hand, and before you know it, you've got that vacation in Acapulco, a second car, or a new kitchen or patio paid for without really feeling the pinch.

Where Did It Go?

● Most people think they can't save because they need every penny. But you'd be surprised how those little extra expenditures can add up. Try this: Write down everything you spend— for your morning coffee, the paper, even a candy bar—in a two-month period. Once you can see, in black and white, where the money is going, you can start to whittle away at the extras and put that money into savings.

Kids can clip coupons for you and earn some money for themselves.

A Penny Not Spent Is a Penny Saved

● Anytime you plan to spend money but don't (you brought your lunch instead of buying it; you borrowed a video from the library instead of renting one from the store), put that money into savings. When you accumulate a large amount, say $500, invest it in bonds or a mutual fund.

● Each week, before you do the grocery shopping, make an entry in your checkbook register in the amount of your usual weekly grocery bill. Then, armed with coupons, rebates, and in-store circulars, shop smarter for the less-expensive generic brands. Put the difference between the final food bill and the actual amount into a savings account.

Smarter Banking

● Look over your bank statements for the last three months and check for service fees. If you find that you're getting charged for checking, ATM fees, and other debits, talk to a representative at your bank and ask about free checking, no-fee ATMs, and the minimum balance you need to maintain in order to avoid penalties. Investigate the option of banking by computer.

● Order your checks from a printer instead of your bank—look in the Yellow Pages or read the mail-order offerings in the Sunday newspaper supplements and in coupon mailers— you'll save more than 50 percent.

● Arrange for your regular monthly

Banking Online

About 4.5 million households in the United States use online banking. Why? It's an inexpensive service—costing as little as $6 a month—and an important part of a good financial management regimen when used with financial software programs. Here are some of the benefits.

● When banking online, a few mouse clicks are all you need to check your account totals, transfer funds, and pay bills. Because your transactions are not subject to the vagaries of the mail, you can time your bill paying so it doesn't outpace your income.

● According to the National Automated Clearing House Association, paying 10 bills a month electronically instead of by check will save you almost $40 a year in stamps, paper checks, and envelopes.

● Software programs can help you create a family budget in a finger snap, figure out how much you can sock away for your children's college education, determine the amount of interest you save by prepaying principal early, and chart a retirement plan.

● When there's a change in your financial situation, either up or down, recalculating your budget takes only a few minutes.

● Computer banking and financial management make tax preparation less taxing.

If you've monitored your electronic downloads for accuracy during the year, your software program should enable you to create reports that will match your transactions to the individual line items on your tax forms, saving you hours adding up stacks of tax-deductible receipts. From there you can fill out your 1040 yourself or send the reports to an accountant. In addition, you should have a program that transfers easily into the most popular tax-preparation programs.

bills to be paid directly out of your bank account. You'll save on postage, late fees, checks, and envelopes.

Small Change

● Here's a way to get your children on the saving bandwagon—and give you some extra time. Pay them a penny for each coupon they clip. Everyone benefits.

● Let your kids see how those coupons and rebates add up—put the savings in an account in their names. It's amazing how enthusiastic they'll become about saving when they see the money accumulating.

● Stash the money you save from coupon clipping in an envelope marked "Fun Money." In a matter of

weeks, you could save enough for a nice dinner out or a weekend away.

Checks and Balances

● When you write a check to a company you haven't done business with before, jot down the address in your checkbook so that it's handy in case you need to check on your order.

The Second Best Thing to Being There

● Keep a stack of prepaid postcards by the telephone. When you're tempted to make a long-distance call, consider jotting a note to that person instead. Or whenever possible, communicate by e-mail . . . you'll be charged for only a local call.

Delay Before You Pay

● Wait at least 24 hours before you make any major purchase. During this time, evaluate whether it is something you really need, how often you intend to use it, and how many hours of work it would take for you to pay for it. You'd be surprised how often a "must-have" turns into a "maybe-not" once you've added up all the facts.

Not Asking Is an Automatic "No"

● It's always worth it to negotiate for a better price or ask for a discount. At worst you'll be told no, but you'll never get any discount if you don't ask.

Entertainment Values

● When you eat out, take advantage of discount coupons and "early-bird" specials. Or order two appetizers as your main entrée. If you've got a large family to feed, limit beverages to water with lemon or lime. The drink tab can add another $20 for a family of five.

● Before your next family vacation, call ahead to a local radio station in the city or cities you'll be visiting and ask if it offers a listener discount card for family specials on dining, entertainment, and accommodations in and around town. This is a great and relatively inexpensive way to enjoy your vacation.

● Negotiate for affordable hotel and motel rates. Call the hotel directly, not the 800 number, and let the person on the phone know that you're calling around for the best rate. Rather than leave a room empty, the hotel will often give it to you at a discount.

● Here's how you can make your entertainment budget go much further—investigate the happenings at your local college or even high school. Weekend sports events, movies, plays, and lectures are much less expensive than their professional counterparts but often just as exciting and enjoyable. And you'll have the added satisfaction

"Specials" and coupons make family meals out affordable.

of knowing that the dollars you spend are supporting education.

● Looking for inexpensive ways to entertain your kids? Many stores offer free activities for children in the hopes that their parents will stay and spend money. Bookstores sometimes have a story hour with guest authors; crafts stores will feature a free "craft of the day." Let your children take advantage of these opportunities, but make it clear that it is a "play," not "pay," day.

Insurance Savings

Asking questions and planning wisely can often save you hundreds of dollars.

HOMEOWNER'S INSURANCE

● Shop around. Prices for identical policies vary as much as 50 percent from company to company. Ask about special rates for preferred customers.

● Choose a high deductible. You're not going to make a claim to replace a $100 window. You want coverage for the big-ticket items. By raising your deductible, you can save up to 25 percent on your premium payment.

● Tailor the policy so it meets your specific needs. If the value of your personal property does not exceed, say, 30 percent of the amount of insurance you carry, you're paying premiums on insurance you may not need.

● Pay your homeowner's premium

Don't overinsure your property— it's money you'll most likely never recoup.

once a year; you may be charged a service fee when you pay in installments.

● Install smoke detectors and burglar alarms. You'll reap a 2 to 5 percent discount.

CAR INSURANCE

● Increase your deductible. Again, it's not the little repairs you want covered, but the big ones.

● Insure all of your cars with one company. You can often get a 15 to 20 percent group discount.

● Take advantage of mature-age discounts. If you're over 50, you may qualify for a discount of up to 20 percent.

● If you have an unblemished driving history, you are eligible for a discount.

● Enroll in a driver-training or defensive-driving course. Each course may save you 10 percent.

● Restrict the number of miles you drive by carpooling or, if possible, by taking advantage of public transportation. If you don't use your car to drive to and from work, most insurers will give you a discount.

● If you're buying a new car, consider antitheft devices and antilock brakes. While these add-ons may cost you more initially, you'll earn a discount from your insurance company for the life of the car.

LIFE INSURANCE

● Consider the options: If you have whole life or universal life insurance policies, replace them with low-cost term insurance. The hidden costs in fees and commissions for whole life and universal policies can cause you to lose up to 30 percent of your money up front.

● Many financial experts believe that life insurance policies make poor investments. You're better off spending less on a no-frills term policy and putting the money you save into a money market account, mutual fund, stocks, or certificate of deposit (CD).

Savings Hot and Cold

● Are you letting your heating and cooling dollars fly out the window? Caulk around doors and windows to reduce costly "air filtration"—when heat escapes and cold air leaks in. Weatherstripping around doors and windows also prevents expensive energy loss. These easy do-it-yourself jobs could reduce your total heating expenses by as much as 6 percent.

● Insulate your attic to "blanket" your house. This prevents rising heat from escaping through your roof. Wrapping insulation around your water heater is another effective way to reduce heat loss and save energy dollars. Your local utility company may offer free home energy inspections and suggest additional ways for you to reduce the cost of heating your home.

● Turn down the thermostat, especially if the house is empty. Invest in a double setback thermostat that can regulate the temperature of your house to coincide with the times it's occupied and empty. For example, during the day when everyone is at work or school, the thermostat can be set at 63 degrees. During the evening hours when everyone is home, it will automatically readjust to a preset temperature of a more comfortable 68 degrees. Then at night, when everyone

Caulking and sealing inefficient windows can reduce your heating and cooling costs.

is tucked in under warm comforters, the temperature again drops down to 63 degrees. Since you save 2 to 3 percent on your energy bill for every degree you lower the thermostat, the two daily setbacks can reduce your yearly heating expenses by as much as 15 to 25 percent.

● Another inexpensive way to reap heating savings: Invest in a humidifier. Moist air retains heat better and is better for you. You can recoup the cost of your initial investment in less than five years.

MAINTAIN OR UPDATE YOUR EQUIPMENT

● Clean and service a gas-fired heating system once a year, an oil-fired system at least twice yearly.

● Replace an old oil-fired heating system with a high-efficiency retention burner, and you may save as much as 20 percent on your heating costs.

● For any heating system (forced air, hot water, steam, or electric), keep the radiators, air registers, and ducts clean, clear of dirt and debris, and free of obstructions such as furniture and draperies.

Use "Lite-Energy" Lights

● Replace some regular lightbulbs in your home with more efficient fluorescents. They last longer and use less energy. Good spots for fluorescents include but are not limited to the garage, workshop, or basement family room.

● It's more cost-effective to turn lights off and on as you need them throughout your

house than to leave lightbulbs burning—and wasting energy—in empty rooms. If you're the forgetful type, you may want install an inexpensive timer device you set to switch your lights off automatically.

Conserve Water

● Take showers. Filling up a tub uses up to twice as much water as the average shower.

● Put a timer device in the bathroom and make sure members of your family—especially teenagers—set it for 10 minutes before getting in the shower.

● Make the most of your 10-minute shower by brushing your teeth and washing out panty hose, delicate socks, and swimsuits at the same time.

● Fix all leaky faucets. Just one drop of water per second dripping from a leaky tap can waste 60 gallons of water a week.

● Install water-conserving showerheads and low-

By switching to more efficient fluorescent lightbulbs, you'll use less energy—and you won't have to change bulbs as often.

water-use toilets. These not only use less water but also prolong the life of your septic system.

● Check the temperature on your water heater. For every 20 degrees you lower the temperature, you reduce your energy cost by 25 percent.

Kitchen Appliance $ense

● Clean the condenser coils on your refrigerator every six months. Dust around the coils makes the motor work harder. You'll use less energy and prolong the life of your refrigerator.

● A full freezer is an efficient freezer, so keep it packed, even with brown paper bags full of ice if necessary. If you don't have a frost-free freezer, defrost it regularly to prevent ice buildup, which makes the freezer less efficient.

● Turn off your dishwasher during the dry cycle and let your dishes air-dry.

● Make sure to clean your microwave oven often. You can do it easily by filling a microwave-safe container with water. Place it in the center of your microwave oven and heat on high for one minute. The steam softens up food particles stuck to the inside of the oven, making them easy to wipe off.

Reining in Holiday Spending

● Save on credit-card interest over the holidays. Buy one gift a week, beginning at least six months before the holiday—and pay cash. Last-minute shopping often forces you to pay more than you intended, and if you charge the gift, you get a double whammy with interest.

● Before you shop, make a detailed master list of everyone you need to buy for and set a spending limit for each gift. If the total is too high, revise your list until it falls within your budget. Don't go shopping until your list is done— and don't leave home without the list.

Giving of your time or sharing a talent can keep your gift budget in balance.

● For large families or office co-workers, suggest having "Secret Santas." Everyone draws one name from the pool and buys a present, within an agreed-upon price range, for that person. Not only will you spend less, but you'll have less shopping to do.

● Another money— and time—saver is to shop at stores that wrap presents for free. You'll spend less on paper, tape, and ribbons.

Keep your food bill consistent by establishing a spending limit.

● Instead of merchandise, why not give a service to friends, family, or co-workers? Offer to make lunch for a week, babysit, or cook, deliver, and serve a fancy dinner. By giving your time, you keep your budget within bounds. And the recipients of these gifts are generally thrilled not to have another dust collector to clean.

● Suggest giving gifts just to the children in your extended family. Most people are relieved to have their shopping lists reduced.

$upermarket $avings

● Look high and low for the best bargains. Supermarket shelves often place the more expensive items at eye level. However, items that appeal to children—sugary cereals and candy— will be placed at their level.

● Definitely clip and use coupons, but don't be tempted to buy something that you wouldn't ordinarily use simply because you have a coupon for it.

● You can save money on meat by buying cuts not marked "lean" and trimming the fat yourself at home.

● Instead of paying more for chicken parts, buy whole fryers and cut them up yourself.

● Buying smaller-size fruit but more pieces gets you through more days of snacks—with fewer calories, too.

● End-of-aisle displays may give the impression that items are discounted, but beware. Often the displays are designed to move merchandise and promote a product without any discount.

● Weigh several bags of vegetables and select the heaviest one. There can be as much as a ¾-pound variation on a 5-pound bag of vegetables.

● Don't pay for what you don't eat— like broccoli stems, for example. Buy broccoli crowns, carrots without tops, and similarly cut vegetables.

●Section II●

YOUR HOME

"Home wasn't built in a day."

Jane Sherwood Ace

Fast and Easy Fix-Its

It's expensive—and aggravating—to have to call a repair person (or nag your significant other) for every little broken thing. A little know-how (plus some help from us) will go a long way toward making your life easier.

With a few essential tools, you can make just about any minor repair.

Little Loose Screw

● Do the screws in your eyeglasses keep coming loose? Put a drop of clear nail polish on the screw after you've retightened it.

● If you have lost a screw in your glasses, here's a temporary fix until you can get them repaired: Use a small safety pin to attach the side piece to the frame.

Tiny Touch-ups

● White liquid correction fluid can be used for small fix-its. Cover up chipped white tile and appliances with the correction fluid. Use it to paint small defects in white moldings. If you need to get a shiny finish, coat the correction fluid with clear nail polish after it dries.

Remove broken lightbulbs safely with a bar of soap.

Backup Earring Back

● Lost the back to an earring? Until you get home, break off a piece of pencil eraser and plunge the post of your earring into it as a temporary backing.

Lights Out

● Here's the safest way to remove a broken lightbulb from a socket. First, turn off the power to that light. Next, take a bar of soap and push it into the open bulb base. Now turn the soap counterclockwise to loosen the remains of the bulb.

● To make it easier to remove a lightbulb when you need to replace it, try this: Prior to screwing the bulb into the socket, rub some petroleum jelly on the threads. This is a particularly useful suggestion for outdoor lights, in which the sockets tend to rust and corrode.

Screen Saver

● You can repair small holes in window and door screens with a touch of clear nail polish.

Painting Pointers

● Use white toothpaste to fill tiny tack holes and imperfections in wall plaster before painting. Allow the toothpaste to dry completely before you begin to paint.

● To keep paint from dripping all over the can when you pour it into a roller tray, punch holes in the can's groove with a hammer and nail. When you pour paint out of the can, the excess will drain back into the can. Make sure you make the holes big enough for the thick paint to drip through.

● Before you begin painting window frames, cut newspaper into strips, dip the strips in water, and press them onto the glass adjacent to the frame. When the paint dries, moisten the newspaper strips with a damp sponge and peel them right off. You won't have messy windowpanes to scrape clean after the painting is done.

● You can also try smearing petroleum jelly on windowpanes, doorknobs, hinges, and other hardware before you begin your paint job. Spatters, drips, and misses will wipe off easily.

● To paint into tiny cracks and crevices in window frames and carved moldings, use a sponge eye-shadow applicator. You'll get great coverage.

● If you do get some paint on windowpanes, a pen eraser does the trick. The abrasive eraser takes off spots quickly and easily and is a lot safer to use than a razor blade.

● Painting baseboards and other low areas? Sit on a skateboard so you can roll along as you paint.

● The area of wall hidden by a switch plate cover is the perfect place to record information about a paint job. Before replacing the switch plate cover, write on the wall the name and

To paint baseboards easily, scoot along the floor sitting on a skateboard.

color of the paint you used and how much of it you needed to paint the room. This takes all the guesswork out of how much paint to buy the next time, and the switch plate cover will conceal your markings.

● Got a really big paint job that will take a few days to complete? Wrap the brush in a piece of aluminum foil to keep it wet at night. This way you clean up only once—when the job is really done.

● If you plan to take a break from painting for a week or so, wrap the roller or brush in aluminum foil, seal it in a plastic bag, and store it in the freezer until you need it.

● At the end of the day, clean your brushes, then rinse in soapy water. To dry, put the handle between both hands and rub your hands to spin off excess water. Wrap the brushes in brown paper to store.

● When painting overhead with a brush, prevent drips on your hands by inserting the handle of the brush through a small paper plate. The paint will drip onto the plate, not onto your hands.

● You don't need to buy a new brush each time you paint. Keep the bristles soft and pliable by cleaning the brush thoroughly, then rubbing some hair conditioner into the bristles before storing it. Be sure to rinse the brush before you use it the next time.

● Get a very tight seal in the paint can by applying a light coat of the paint in the grooves at the top of the can. When you tap the lid shut, the paint will create a seal for better storage of the paint, but it will be easy to reopen the can the next time you use it.

● Wear a 30-gallon garbage bag as a coverall when you're painting overhead. Cut a hole in the top of the bag for your head and two holes in the sides for your arms. To protect your head, wear a disposable plastic shower cap. Toss everything when you're done painting.

● Another option: Wear your clothes inside out. If you do get some paint on them, your clothes won't be ruined.

● Or designate some old outfit as your "painting ensemble." Stow these clothes with your painting equipment so you're sure to wear them when you start a job.

● Before painting outdoor concrete steps, add a small amount of store-bought sand to the can of paint. When the steps are dry, they will be slightly rough in texture, better for nonskid footing.

● If you're painting over wood and you don't want the knots to show through, first apply some wood filler to the knots; allow to dry thoroughly. Then apply either varnish or a spray-on stain killer specifically made to seal knots (both are available at hardware stores). Allow to dry completely, then paint.

● Replace picture hooks with thumbtacks before you paint a wall. Paint over the tack and then remove it once the wall is dry. Now you can replace the hook in the same hole.

● When you're painting a cabinet door, press a few pushpins into the frame to prevent the door from closing completely while the paint is drying.

● If painter's masking tape won't come off easily, warm it with a hair dryer to loosen the adhesive.

● You can still smell a newly painted room for days after you've painted. To reduce or eliminate the odor, leave a dish filled with white vinegar in the room while you work.

● Or rub some vanilla extract on the incandescent lightbulbs in the room. When the lights are on, the heat releases the just-baked scent and masks the new-paint odor. (Don't put extract on halogen bulbs—it will burn.)

● Cleanups after painting with oil-base paint can be nasty. Instead of using paint thinner on your body, use vegetable oil, which is safer, is mild on delicate skin, and has no fumes. This is an especially good idea for any children who have gotten into the paint.

● Keep a small amount of paint for each room in an empty, clean nail polish bottle. If you need to do a minor touch-up, you'll have the paint—and brush—right at your fingertips.

Wallpaper Hang-ups?

● Can't get old wallpaper off the wall? Try this: Fill a spray bottle with a solution of two-thirds hot water and one-third liquid fabric softener. Saturate the wallpaper with the solution, beginning at the top and along the seams. Wait 20 minutes and then carefully peel the paper off the wall. Respray the wall as needed. Keep the solution warm by immersing the spray bottle in a pot of hot water between sprayings.

● Mix wallpaper paste with a large kitchen whisk to eliminate lumps.

● Add a tiny bit of food coloring to wallpaper paste so it's more visible on the walls when you apply it.

● Use a paint roller to apply wallpaper paste directly to the walls. It's easier to cover a large area and it goes on evenly, with fewer lumps and bumps.

● A large cooler makes an ideal soaking tub for prepasted wallpaper. Fill it with a few inches of water and your precut wallpaper fits right inside.

● Make it easy on yourself when you hang wallpaper. If you're right-handed, work left to right. If you're a lefty, work right to left.

Furniture Fix-ups

● If a wooden dresser drawer keeps sticking, it's most likely because moisture has expanded the wood. To correct the problem, empty out the drawer and place a safety light with a 60-watt incandescent bulb inside the open drawer for 20 minutes. The heat from the lamp will dry up the moisture, and the drawer should glide easily again.

● To further improve the drawer's slide-ability, apply a thin layer of paste wax to the outer sides and bottom of the drawer and to the glider on the inside of the dresser.

● If a screw hole in wood furniture becomes too large to hold the screw, try this: Remove the screw and pack

A 60-watt bulb can shrink a sticky drawer back to its original size.

the hole with toothpicks and wood glue. Wait for the glue to dry, then trim the toothpicks even with the surface. Redrill the hole and replace the screw. For larger holes, use wooden chopsticks or slender wooden dowels.

● A dab of matching shoe polish can fill in minor nicks and scratches in wood. In some cases a touch of brown marker does the trick. Allow either to dry thoroughly before polishing.

● To touch up scratches on dark wood furniture, mix instant coffee and a bit of water to form a paste and rub it on the scratches. Furniture will look like new.

● Glue small pieces of felt, cork, or adhesive-backed bunion pads to the bottoms of pots, vases, and other items that can mar or scratch tabletops.

● Got a water ring on your favorite wood coffee table? Apply a "mayonnaise plaster" to the stain. Saturate the area with mayonnaise, then cover it with a soft, lint-free cloth and put a book on top to make sure the mayonnaise penetrates the wood's finish. The oil from the mayonnaise helps eliminate the telltale mark.

Wood Wonders

● To tell if a piece of wood you've sanded is completely smooth, put an old nylon panty hose over your hand and run your hand over the sanded surface. The nylon will snag on any rough spots or imperfections in the wood.

● To fill a gouge in a wood floor, take a crayon that matches the color of the wood, melt it in a microwave oven,

pour it into the gouge, and smooth the surface. After the crayon hardens, wax the floor. This trick works for vinyl floors too.

Squeak Relief

● Wood floors creaky? Sprinkle some talcum powder between the floorboards. This will fill in the tiny gaps caused by shrinkage and imperfections in the wood.

Squeaky wood floors? A touch of talcum powder should silence them.

● Noisy door hinges driving you crazy? A spritz of vegetable oil cooking spray or a bit of oil lubricating spray, such as WD-40, should take care of it.

Dust-Free Electronics

● Renovating the rooms in your home is dusty business, to be sure. To keep telephones, answering machines, VCRs, and other electronic devices visible, usable, and dust-free, enclose them in large self-sealing plastic bags before the work begins.

No-Slammer Hammer

● If you are unable to hammer a nail without hammering your fingers in the process, use the tines of an old fork—instead of your fingers—to hold the nail in place.

Hammer It Home

● Here's how to hammer in a nail without splitting a plaster or drywall surface: Drop the nail into a pot of hot water for 15 seconds; drain, remove carefully, and hammer in. The heated nail softens some of the surrounding plaster before penetrating it, thus preventing cracks and splits.

● Another way to keep plaster from chipping when you drill or hammer into it is to cover the area with transparent tape before you start.

● Never drive two nails into the same grain line—it will cause the wood to split. Instead, be sure to stagger nails along the grain of the board.

● Here's another way to reduce the chances a nail will split wood—blunt the tip of the nail first by tapping it lightly with the hammer.

Stubborn Screw

● To remove a stubborn screw, pass a lighted match over the end of the screwdriver. The heated tip will expand slightly and fit more snugly in the groove of the screw, making it easier to twist out.

● Or apply vinegar, peroxide, or lubricating oil to help loosen a rusty or stubborn screw.

● To make it easier to insert a screw into wood, rub the screw shank across a candle stub, a bar of soap, or beeswax. (Beeswax doesn't leave any stain, so choose it if you are screwing into a spot that's visible.)

If your aim with a hammer is a little rusty, use a fork—instead of fingers—to hold the nail in place.

TLC for Tools

● Keep moisture from rusting expensive house and garden tools by placing one or two pieces of charcoal in your toolbox.

● Wrap tool handles with electrician's tape to improve the grip and keep padded handles from wearing out.

● Another way to keep rust from forming on small garden tools: Coat the metal with oil, then plunge the lubricated tool into a sand-filled pail.

A well-stocked toolbox can meet most ordinary carpentry needs.

Toolbox Basics

With these in your toolbox, you can take on basic building projects.

GEAR NECESSITIES

Dust mask, knee pads, safety goggles, utility belt, work gloves (one canvas or leather pair, one rubber pair, and a box of disposables).

MANUAL MUST-HAVES

Clamp To hold items to work surface.

Curved-claw hammer 16-ounce with a drop-forged, heavy-duty steel head. When hammering, use your whole arm, not just your wrist, to drive nails. Always wear eye protection to guard against flying wood splinters and nails.

Hand saw Full size (20 to 24 inches). Invest in a high-quality saw; those with more teeth per inch provide a smoother cut. The wood to be sawed should be clamped to a worktable at a comfortable height.

Metal tape measure Retractable, at least 25 feet long.

Sandpaper In fine, medium, and coarse grits.

Screwdrivers Two slotted (flat-head), one blade ¼-inch wide, the other ³⁄₁₆-inch; two Phillips head, sizes #1 and #2. The larger the handle, the more torque (twisting power) you have and the less chance for slips.

Slip-joint pliers To grip nuts, pull nails, or cut or twist wire.

Spirit level 12 to 24 inches long.

Utility knife With retractable blade for safety.

Wrench Adjustable to 10 inches, to loosen and tighten nuts and bolts. Adjust to fit tightly to the nut. Don't use on a rounded-corner nut; it can slip.

Safety Tips Buy tools with rubber or vinyl coating to improve grip and prevent electrical shock. Never leave tools anywhere other than in your utility belt or toolbox while working. Make sure all cutting tools are sharp.

POWER SQUADRON

Circular saw Makes straight cuts only, goes quickly through heavy lumber (2 x 4s and 2 x 6s). Blade should be carbide-tipped, hardened steel with a retractable guard. Have blades professionally sharpened when necessary. Keep bottom of saw clean and free of rust.

Cordless drill Choose a ⅜-inch reversible-speed model that's strong enough to drive through 2 inches of wood. A 9.6- or 12-volt drill should do. The drill chuck holds bits in a range of sizes, plus other accessories, such as a circular disk for sanding. A keyless chuck saves time when switching bits.

Handheld jigsaw Light, easy to handle; makes straight and curved cuts. Some models offer blade options and variable speeds.

Router with assorted bits Makes grooves, edges. For deep cuts, you may need to make more than one pass.

Safety Tips Read instruction manual thoroughly before using any power tool. Never use near water. Plug into outlets protected with ground-fault circuit interrupters (GFCIs). Do not wear loose, dangling clothing that could get caught in moving parts. When sawing, set blade depth only a quarter inch more than the thickness of the material being cut, and make sure power cords are out of the way. Support material properly so it will not pinch blade, causing it to kick back toward you. Wear eye and ear protection. Use extension cords designed for power tools (12- or 14-gauge wire). If tool has a third prong, make sure extension cord also has a third prong. Always unplug tools when adjusting or changing bits and blades.

PAINTING PARAPHERNALIA

Brushes 1- to 2½-inch angled brushes, 2- to 4-inch straight brushes, different sizes of foam brushes. Invest in high-quality brushes; natural bristles for alkyd paints, synthetic for water-base paints; use foam for touch-ups.

Drop cloths To cover floors, furniture.

Paint stirrers Free at paint stores.

Paint trays and buckets For small areas, use trays with disposable liners. For large areas, use 5-gallon buckets fitted with wire racks.

Painter's masking tape Brown paper tape (with one adhesive edge) and blue masking tape, both in assorted widths.

Rollers 9- to 11-inch roller handles with sleeves. For small areas, 4- to 6-inch foam rollers with covered tips.

Scraper 4-inch razor blade or wall scraper.

Wire brush To scrape off flaking paint or rust.

Safety Tips Do not remove lead paint yourself. Doing so improperly can cause lead particles to disperse throughout your house. Hire a professional.

Keep drains clog-free with baking soda and vinegar.

Plumbing Problem Primer

You can prevent little leaks from becoming big drains on your wallet with these simple, do-it-yourself fix-its.

CLOGGED DRAINS?

● Kitchen sink drain sluggish or clogged? Pour boiling hot water down the drain. If grease is preventing the flow of water, the hot water will melt the grease and open up the drain.

● If hot water isn't enough to clear your sink, use a plunger to unstop the drain. To get a solid seal in the drain, hold the plunger directly perpendicular to the sink and then give it three or four good pumps to dislodge the clump.

● To prevent those nasty sink clog-ups in the first place, never pour grease or greasy by-products down the drain. Instead, keep an empty cardboard milk carton next to the sink for just such a purpose. Place the carton in the freezer between uses, seal shut, and place in the garbage when full.

● About once a month, pour ¼ cup baking soda into your sink and tub drains, followed by just enough warm water to get the powder down into the drains. Next, pour 1 cup white vinegar down the drain. Let the mixture sit for 3 to 12 hours to dissolve bacteria buildup in the pipe drains and traps (the U-shaped section of pipe). Flush the mixture through the drains the next day with hot water.

Prevention Tip Place drain screens, available at most hardware and grocery stores, in the kitchen and bathroom sinks, bathtub, and shower. These will prevent typical drain cloggers—food particles, hair, soap slivers, toothpaste caps—from getting into the pipes.

LEAKY FAUCET?

● Don't let the drip-drip-drip drive you crazy. Chances are, the washer needs to be replaced. Here's how to do it:

1. Turn off the main water valve under the sink.

2. Open the faucet to drain out the water from the pipes.

3. Unscrew the setscrew on the handle. Remove the handle.

4. Using an open-end wrench, unscrew the stem, then remove it.

5. Remove the screw that holds the washer to the bottom of the stem. Replace the washer. Tighten the screw back on firmly without damaging the washer.

6. Replace the stem and screw in. Replace the handle.

Prevention Tip Turn the faucet off but don't tighten the handle any more than is needed to stop the water. Overtightening the handles wears down the washers.

A plunger coated with petroleum jelly is more effective.

TOILET TROUBLE?

● Toilet stopped up? Don't panic, you most likely can fix it yourself. Here's what to do:

1. If the water in your toilet bowl is rising past its normal level, remove the top of the tank and flip the rubber stopper in the bottom of the tank back over the drain hole. This will stop the flow of water into the bowl.

2. Pour a solution of 1 cup liquid bleach, 1 cup liquid detergent, and 1 gallon hot water down the drain. Let it stand for 20 minutes. This should help break up paper products that may be stuck in the drain.

Remove old, dirty-looking caulk and replace with a fresh application.

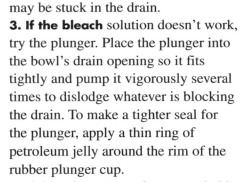

3. If the bleach solution doesn't work, try the plunger. Place the plunger into the bowl's drain opening so it fits tightly and pump it vigorously several times to dislodge whatever is blocking the drain. To make a tighter seal for the plunger, apply a thin ring of petroleum jelly around the rim of the rubber plunger cup.

4. If that doesn't work, you probably *do* need a plumber. Don't take it upon yourself to pour chemicals down the toilet or use a rubber snake, which could damage pipes. A plumber will determine the next best step. If you have already used chemicals, make sure to alert the plumber so his skin doesn't come in contact with them. Also, the plumber may use a chemical drain cleaner, and you don't want to risk the combination of chemicals creating a deadly mix.

Prevention Tip Once a month, pour brewer's yeast and sugar down the toilet bowl drain. When mixed with

water, the sugar activates the yeast, which in turn starts to "eat" away at microbes and bacteria in the septic tank or cesspool.

Caulk Talk

● Dry, yellowed, or mildewed caulking can make a clean bathroom look dirty. To replace cracked or unsightly caulking, follow these simple steps:

1. Use a stiff putty knife and craft knife or other small, sharp blade to remove all the old caulking material around the tub. Get out as much of the old caulking material as possible.

2. Scrub the entire area with a bleach-based cleanser and a stiff brush. Rinse well and allow it to dry completely before proceeding to the next step.

3. Purchase latex-based tub-and-tile caulk in either a squeeze tube or a caulking gun and apply a thin, continuous bead of caulk to the shallow groove where the old caulking used to be. Use the least amount of caulk possible to fill in the gap. Excess caulk that hangs over the tub or tile can actually become a moisture trap that allows mildew to grow.

4. Before the caulk starts to form a skin and harden—usually within a few minutes—moisten your fingertip and use it to smooth out the caulking and fill in any gaps. Tip: For extra-smooth caulking, use an ice cube instead of your fingertip to spread the caulk.

5. Wipe away excess caulk with a damp cloth. Allow the caulking to dry according to product instructions.

Steam Away

● Install an exhaust fan with exterior ventilation in the bathroom to keep humidity down. Choose an exhaust fan with an appropriate CFM (cubic feet per minute) rating. This is the rate at which the fan can exchange air. To determine the correct CFM for your bathroom, multiply the square footage of your bathroom by 1.07. If the ceilings are high, select a fan with a greater CFM than indicated.

Black Spot Not

● Wipe down the tub and shower stall completely after each use. By keeping moisture to a minimum, you prevent mildew from forming. A rubber squeegee makes this job easy.

● An open window in the bathroom also helps prevent mildew by allowing steam and moisture to escape and surfaces to air-dry faster.

Glue News

● Soften glue with warm distilled white vinegar. Just add a drop or two of the vinegar to the glue, then stir.

● Keep lids on glue bottles and tubes easy to take off and put on. Before recapping, apply a small bit of petroleum jelly to the threads.

● Store glue bottles upside down to make it easier to pour and squeeze the glue the next time you need it.

GLUES TO USE

The three types of glue listed here can take care of nearly all of your gluing needs. You'll find them at any hardware store or home center.

Epoxy Use epoxy to bond dissimilar surfaces, such as glass to wood, or plastic to metal. It's waterproof, rigid, and very strong.

Polyvinyl acetate Fancy name for the familiar white glue in a squeeze bottle. It dries clear and strong and is good for interior use on wood, paper, and ceramics.

Polyvinyl chloride Use this glue to repair broken china. It also adheres to marble, wood, or metal.

Savvy Storage Solutions

Besides time, the one thing most people never have enough of is space. It's a law of physics: Nature abhors a vacuum. This is no better exemplified than in most people's closets. Our storage solutions will show you how to find more space in *every* room of the house. The trick is, once you've found more space, how are you going to keep from filling it up again?

Closets filling up faster than you can empty them? Don't despair—you have more room than you think.

Bedroom Bonanza

● To reduce the clutter of earrings on a dresser, here's a practical—and pretty—solution. Remove the glass from a freestanding picture frame and replace it with a piece of metal window screen, cut to fit. Now you can hang your earrings so they stay organized and easy to find.

● To expand your closet's capacity instantly, create a double level by installing a second rod just below the bottoms of your hanging shirts.

● Install towel bars on the back of your closet door. Two bars fit very nicely and are great for hanging pants and scarves.

● Where do you stash the clothes you intend to take to the dry cleaner? Don't drape them over furniture or pile them in the corner of the room. Instead, buy or make a large drawstring bag and hang it on the back of a closet door. Toss the clothes into the bag, and when you're ready to take them to the cleaner, just grab the bag and go. No more searching through your closet for soiled clothing.

● Arrange your clothes in the closet in a way that's useful to you—work clothes together, casual clothes together. Buy all the same type of hangers—wooden or tubular—and hang them so they face the same direction.

● Get your shoes off the floor. If you have a standard closet, place your shoes on the shelf above the rod, then build another shelf above them. Or buy a hanging bag that enables you to sort shoes.

● Place an empty dish drainer rack on a clothes closet shelf to make a great storage basket for purses.

Display your everyday earrings on a freestanding picture frame—pretty and practical.

Linens 'n' Things

● Sew strips of hook-and-loop fastener on the open end of an old pillowcase and use it to wrap blankets and the like for storage during the off-season.

● Remove the bottom two shelves of a linen closet and install a rod for hanging tablecloths and linens.

Nursery Know-how

● Here's a tip to help you maximize storage space when you have a new baby. Keep three laundry baskets under the baby's crib for toys, extra blankets, diapers, and related items. The baskets slide out easily when you need them and are hidden by the crib's ruffle when you don't.

● What to do with the plethora of plush toys in your little one's room? Hang a bright-colored plastic-coated chain from the ceiling and suspend plush toys from the chain with colorful clothespins. Not only does it make the room neater, but it serves as a pretty neat decoration too.

● Use empty infant-wipe containers to store miniature cars, doll clothes, hair accessories, and other assorted items. You can write on the containers with indelible markers to identify the contents. Best of all, the containers are free!

> In the playroom, keep storage bins and shelves at a kid-friendly height.

Kids' Corner

● Set up a children's corner somewhere in your house where toys, books, games, and projects can be stowed at the end of the day. Make sure cubbies, shelves, and storage bins are at a height that is kid-friendly and easy—as well as safe—to open and close.

● Invest in adjustable shelving units for kids' rooms and closets so that the shelves can be raised or added as the kids grow.

Dining Room Details

● To free up needed drawer space in the dining room, clip place mats and tablecloths onto a multiple skirt hanger and put the hanger in the entry closet. The place mats and tablecloths will always be neat and wrinkle-free.

● Stacking chairs are an excellent investment. When you need more room, you can stack them in a corner or closet.

● Store your everyday dishes and flatware in a small wheeled cart near the dining table.

Garage Gadgets

● An old golf bag makes an excellent storage caddy for long-handled tools, like rakes, hoes, and shovels.

● Long-handled tools can also be stored in large garbage cans with wheels. The cans hold a lot of equipment, and you can wheel them to wherever you're working in the yard.

● Redoing a kitchen? Don't toss out those old cabinets. Install them in the garage to use for storage of paints, chemicals, and other things. Write or affix labels on the outside of each cabinet to indicate the contents.

● Old kitchen countertops can also be recycled and used as workbenches in a garage or basement. For a temporary setup, place the old countertop on two sawhorses. For a more permanent workbench, place atop old floor-mounted kitchen cabinets; build or buy a sturdy base for the countertop; or affix it to the wall with sturdy steel brackets.

Hobby Helper

● To store your notions, put a lazy Susan on your sewing table. Everything you need is just a spin away.

Double-Duty Furniture

● It's a coffee table. Or is it? Trunks, baskets, and blanket chests make terrific coffee tables, and they have lots of storage space inside.

● Cover a filing cabinet with a pretty cloth and place mat or a table topper and voilà! A useful and attractive end table.

● Want to create a window seat—and gain some stowaway space at the same time? Purchase a large wicker basket with a lid and place pillows or a large cushion on top.

● Cover a small heavy-duty storage bin with fabric to create an attractive ottoman. Use the bin to store things you want near you when you relax— reading material, sewing or crafts projects, crossword puzzles.

Walls That Work

● Position a drop-leaf table against the wall. The drop leaf can be flipped up when you need the space, lowered for more room when you don't.

● Hang baskets and other small containers from walls. For example, affix a small container on the wall near the phone to hold pens, paper, or address book. There's no need to put holes in the wall. Just use self-adhesive hook-and-loop fastener dots to hold the container in place. The room will seem bigger, cleaner, and airier when there's less clutter on the countertops and other surfaces.

Choose furniture that does double-duty as storage bins.

● String lengths of raffia, ribbon, or decorative cord horizontally along the wall. Using colorful clothespins, attach memos, notes, or children's artwork.

Living Room

● You can never have enough bookcases—not just for storing books but for displaying decorative objects. Don't skimp on bookcase size. You'll never be sorry if you put floor-to-ceiling bookcases against as many walls as you can.

● To store vases or other attractive items, be on the lookout for "dead space" between the ceiling and the top of a cabinet or hutch. These instantly transform into display spaces.

● Buy or build corner cabinets and shelving. Corners are often overlooked in a room, but filling in these areas is an efficient use of space in any room.

● Skirt a table. A graceful covering for a side table can hide boxes of odds and ends, such as greeting cards, craft supplies, and photographs waiting to be put into scrapbooks.

Kitchen in Sync

● Get rid of those bulky boxes in pantry closets by repackaging their contents—cereals, pastas, crackers—into resealable plastic bags or other space-saving, see-through containers.

● Do you really need to stow all those cookbooks in the kitchen when you use only a few recipes from each one? Consider this option: Make copies of the recipes you use and place them in a magnetic photo album—the kind with

Storage Rules to Live by

● Thinking of buying something? Before the purchase, think about where you will store it.

● When you do bring something new into your house, make it a point to throw out or give away something old. This holds true for anything you might acquire—toys, shoes, tools, dishes, kitchen gadgets, linens, umbrellas, games, furniture.

● The saying "A place for everything and everything in its place" is key. Don't think of just a general place, such as "in the kitchen." Be specific: "The drawer next to the sink in the third compartment." The more exact the place is for each item, the more likely you'll be to put it back. Also, it's easier to spot when something's missing when you've designated just one spot to keep it in.

● Organize and store items in places convenient to their use. Arrange frequently used items on waist-to-eye-level shelves, drawers, or hooks; seldom-used items up high or down low.

plastic sleeves over the pages. You can then move those bulky cookbooks elsewhere or sell them at your next garage sale.

● When you need extra space here, look *up!* Build a high shelf around the perimeter of the kitchen to store seldom-used cookware, dishes, or decorative pitchers.

● If your ceilings are high enough, hang a pot rack in the kitchen and from it suspend the pots and pans you use most often.

● To free up drawer space, install a magnetic strip on the back of a cabinet door and use it to hang knives.

● Display wire whisks, spatulas, and other large cooking utensils in a pretty container on the kitchen counter.

● Install a shelf across the back wall of a deep cabinet as a means of elevating some items; use the space beneath the shelf to store others.

● Stow things you use daily in top drawers, on easily reached shelves, or under the sink. Things you need infrequently (seasonal and items for special occasions) can go on the top of shelves and in some base cabinets.

● Need extra counter space in your kitchen? Have a solid piece of wood cut to fit into your sink or across a drawer to give you an extra cutting surface.

● Keep all surfaces as free of clutter as possible. Display only what you use often, and stash everything else.

● Leave small everyday appliances, such as the toaster or coffeemaker, on the countertops. Put away those used less frequently—perhaps the slow cooker or blender.

Surprise! 5 Storage Spaces You Didn't Know You Had

High Ceiling
Ceiling space—especially extra-high ceilings—can be the answer to the storage-starved's prayers. In a basement, attic, or garage, mount racks to stow seasonal items—skis, fishing poles, sports equipment. In an alcove or above a doorway, you can create a closet overhead from some of that dead air space. This requires some carpentry skill (or you can have someone build it for you to your specifications). This space can be ideal for storing blankets, seasonal items such as decorations, or old files.

Basement or Attic Stair Wall
The wall leading down to the basement or up to the attic is a storage bonanza. Suspend a grid or Peg-Board on the wall and use it to hang dust mops and pans, feather dusters, handheld vacuum, or iron. Or if you can, build recessed shelves into the wall leading down to your basement and store pantry items there. With the extra room, you'll be able to stock up on bulk items available from a warehouse-type shopping club.

Beneath the Stairs
The space beneath a staircase may provide unexpected storage possibilities. If it is enclosed or if you can put a cupboard in it, use the space to stow seasonal items, such as holiday decorations, athletic equipment, and extra blankets and pillows. In some cases you might be able to eke out a small office or desk space beneath the stairs.

Fireplace
Do you use your fireplace every month of the year? Most of us don't. When not in use, the fireplace is a great space for storage. Buy some attractive baskets with lids that will fit just inside the opening, and stow magazines, games, or other nonessentials inside. A pretty plant—real or fake—placed with the baskets makes the space more inviting. Or mask the opening with a decorative fire screen.

Old Suitcases
Old suitcases are great for storing almost anything—from holiday decorations to photo albums. Label the suitcases and store them in your basement, attic, garage, or closet. A bonus: They're easy to retrieve—just grab one by the handle and you're off.

• Turn the lost space above your kitchen cabinets into storage space by installing sliding or winged doors.

• Save space in a pantry closet by nesting empty plastic storage containers. Place the lids in a resealable plastic bag and hang the bag from a hook inside the door. You won't have to fumble around for either, and the closet stays much neater.

• Attach easy-to-install holders (like paper-towel racks) on the inside of the cabinet door for foil and plastic wrap.

• You don't have a broom closet? Attach hooks to the back of the basement or closet door instead. Hang brooms, mops, iron, ironing board. They're all out of sight when the doors are closed and easy to retrieve when you need them. Look for clamping holders and other special devices at a closet shop.

Odds and Ends

• Those plastic zippered covers that new blankets come in are perfect for storing decorative wreaths.

• Empty liquor bottle cases make excellent storage boxes for Christmas ornaments. Each bottle compartment holds one or two ornaments.

• Got lots of pretty things you'd like to display but no more usable surface space? Build a display shelf or box above a window.

Bathroom Basics

• Install shelves in the large cavity below the sink and use them to store tissue, soap, and cleaning supplies.

• No vanity beneath your bathroom sink? Affix one half of a strip of hook-and-loop tape to the outside of the sink and the other half to some pretty fabric; then hang the fabric to hide pipes and give you an extra storage spot. You can even put a rolling bin under the space to stash extra toilet paper, soap, or shampoo.

• Put a wine rack in your bathroom next to the tub—even paint the rack to coordinate with your decor. Then roll up clean towels and place them in the rack. A pretty and practical solution to towel storage.

• Take advantage of empty space above the toilet by adding a small cabinet or shelves for extra linens or toiletries. Freestanding over-the-commode shelves can maximize this space right up to the ceiling.

• A second shower curtain rod, added behind and level with the first, provides a handy place to hang wet

A wine rack is a clever way to stow—and display—bathroom towels.

towels so they can air-dry before you fold and return them to the rack. If you have glass shower doors in your bathroom and there is no place to install a shower rod, consider replacing wall towel racks with hooks—you'll be able to hang more towels in the same space.

● Organize your medicine cabinet with the items you use daily (such as deodorant and shaving cream) on the lower shelf; those you need less often on the top shelf.

● No room for a clothes hamper in your bathroom? Think again. Squeeze one into the space between the toilet and the sink or between the toilet and the tub. If you can't find a traditional hamper to fit that space, try an alternative—a tall plastic kitchen garbage can, for instance.

The Illusion of Space

● A folding screen can create a separate space where none now exists. Use it to hide an office setup, exercise "room," or sewing center. A row of tall potted plants also makes a natural screen that still gives a room an "open" feel.

A "screen" of green plants divides a large space into workable rooms.

● Hang a mirror on a wall opposite the window to create the illusion of more room, even if you can't squeeze out another square inch of extra space. But keep things neat near the mirror. You may get the illusion of more space, but you'll also double the amount of clutter if you leave a mess.

● Or hang a print or painting of an outdoor scene on an interior wall. Give the appearance of a window by hanging a mirrored window frame on a wall and adorning your new "window" with curtains.

● Make an ordinary window look recessed—and give yourself some added storage space—by building bookcases around, beneath, and above the window.

● Put a wide hallway to use. Place a small desk there to hold papers, or a table covered with a pretty cloth to hide storage underneath.

An A-to-Z Clean Everything Faster, Easier Guide

From appliance grime to zinc oxide stains, we'll tell you how to breeze through your cleaning.

Cleaning. It's a dirty job, and sooner or later, everyone's got to do it. But you don't have to clean up the hard way. We've amassed the best tips and hints and organized them in easy-to-refer-to alphabetical order to make the most dreaded household chores a "no sweat" proposition. Good luck!

A

Air Conditioners

● Tape dryer fabric-softener sheets over your air-conditioner filter. This will give the house a fresh smell and make the filter last longer.

● Wall units will operate more efficiently if you clean the filters regularly. To do so, unplug the air conditioner, then remove the cover panel or grille. Place the grille in a sink full of soapy warm water and scrub the louvers clean with a scrub brush. Rinse, then set aside to dry. Wrap a putty knife in a cleaning cloth to dry between the slats. Remove the foam filter and gently wash it in a solution of warm water and disinfectant (to remove mold and mildew spores). Gently rinse until the water runs clear, then carefully squeeze out the excess water. When dry, reassemble the unit.

Aluminum Doors

● Just spray dirt and grime off your aluminum storm door with whitewall tire cleaner.

Appliances

● To remove handprints from an appliance, clean with a soft cloth dampened with rubbing alcohol. It leaves surfaces clean, shiny, and streak-free.

● Polish and then buff both the inside and outside of your refrigerator with car wax. It will look new, and spills, stains, and fingerprints will wipe off easily.

● At least every few months, clean behind your heavy appliances. To make moving them easier, slide a towel or cotton scatter rug under the two weight-bearing legs. This also helps prevent scratches on flooring. With the refrigerator unplugged, vacuum the condenser coils. Use a narrow brush to clean under the stove or fridge. Clean the walls and floors behind the unit, then slide it back into place and replug.

● Clean an automatic drip coffeemaker by running vinegar through it.

● Use oven cleaner on the outside of your toaster and other chrome appliances. Place the appliance on an old dishtowel, spray on the cleaner, wait 5 minutes, and then wipe with a clean cloth.

● Apply a very thin coat of petroleum jelly to your refrigerator door gasket to protect it from mildew, drying, and cracking and to improve the seal.

Handprints happen, but rubbing alcohol makes them vanish.

Here's a smart way to clean your electric can opener: Soak an old toothbrush in vinegar, hold it under the blade, and turn on the machine.

To keep stainless-steel stoves and black glass-front appliances looking like new, wipe them down with rubbing alcohol on a lint-free cloth.

After you're through defrosting the freezer, spray a few coats of nonstick cooking spray on the ceiling and sides of the freezer. The next time you defrost, the ice will fall right off.

To test if the gasket around your refrigerator is in good condition, try this: Close the refrigerator door on a dollar bill, leaving a small corner sticking out. If you are able to pull the bill out easily, the gasket is not creating an airtight seal. You must either replace the gasket or adjust the hinges on the door so it fits tighter.

Ashtrays

To remove nicotine residue from ashtrays, wipe them out with a paper towel dampened with rubbing alcohol.

Better yet, fill decorative ashtrays with potpourri to discourage guests from smoking in your house.

B
Barbecue Grills

Use a cloth soaked in vegetable oil to remove ashes and polish the outside of a grill. The grill must be hot for the oil to work as a polish, so use very heavy oven mitts to protect your hands.

Keep grill grates clean by applying a coat of oil every time you barbecue.

When you're finished cooking, scrub the grates with a metal wire brush. (Leave a gas grill on while doing this.) Reapply the oil.

Baseball Caps

Baseball caps come clean in the top rack of your dishwasher—and they don't lose their shape.

Bathroom

Mineral oil removes soap scum from fiberglass shower doors quickly and easily. Next time you take a shower, note how the water runs right off.

To keep the bathroom mirror fog-free after a shower, clean it regularly with shaving cream instead of glass cleaner.

Shower gel or liquid soap will clean your tub and prevent ugly soap scum buildup.

Here's a way to clean—and polish—bathroom tile: Instead of regular tile cleaner, use a polish made for fiberglass products (like boat hulls and outdoor furniture). The compound and wax combination in the polish removes soap scum, and the wax leaves behind a protective coating that helps prevent water spotting and mildew formation, making future cleanups a breeze.

Use a little bit of baby shampoo on a wet sponge to clean the bathroom sink, tub, and tiles. Shampoo cuts right through dirt and oily residue, leaving behind a fresh scent.

Drop a denture cleaning tablet into your toilet bowl, allow it to sit for several hours, then flush. This removes stains without the need for using any elbow grease or even your hands.

● If you run out of tub and tile cleaner for the bathroom, try a bit of toothpaste on a wet cloth. Rub the paste in and then rinse. Your whole bathroom will sparkle, shine, and smell minty fresh too!

● Used dryer fabric-softener sheets are really great for removing ugly soap scum from glass shower doors. They don't leave behind any lint, and the softener residue on the sheets helps prevent future soap buildup.

● Here's a sneaky way to curb excess moisture in your bathroom: Hide a few pieces of coal in an obscure corner.

Toothpaste makes a minty fresh tile cleaner.

Coal absorbs moisture and odor too.

● Turn on the hot water in the shower 10 minutes before you're ready to clean the bathroom. The steam will soften any mold and mildew.

● After you've thoroughly cleaned the tiles in your bathroom, spray on a light coat of ordinary car wax, then buff them. The next time you take a shower, you'll find that the water will run right off the surface.

● To prevent cans from leaving a rust ring on your medicine cabinet shelves and on countertops, coat the bottom rim of the metal with a bit of clear nail polish.

Kids Can Help

Many hands make light work. Let kids get in on the cleaning act. You'll be teaching them valuable life skills, empowering them with "important" work, and lessening the load on yourself. Here's an age-appropriate breakdown.

AGES 2 TO 3	AGES 4 TO 5	AGES 6 TO 8	AGES 9 TO 13
✔ Put toys in bin. ✔ Fill pet's bowl. ✔ Put clothes in hamper.	✔ Stack newspapers. ✔ Sort or help fold laundry; match socks. ✔ Dust table legs and chair legs. ✔ Empty wastebaskets.	✔ Load and unload dishwasher. ✔ Make own snacks or lunch. ✔ Sweep and damp-mop floors. ✔ Put away clothes. ✔ Dust table surfaces. ✔ Wash bathroom sink and tub.	✔ Clean refrigerator. ✔ Put away groceries. ✔ Load and unload washer and dryer with presorted garments. ✔ Straighten and organize linens. ✔ Iron clothes. ✔ Vacuum all carpets. ✔ Wipe mirrors and wash windows. ✔ Polish furniture. ✔ Dust lampshades. ✔ Clean tiles and toilet with disinfectant. ✔ Wipe shower doors.

Is lime deposit buildup making your showerhead less efficient? Pour a few tablespoons of red or white vinegar into a small—but sturdy—plastic bag, then fasten the bag securely around your showerhead; let the showerhead soak for a couple of hours. The acid in the vinegar will clear away the mineral deposits that clogged the showerhead.

Keep your bathroom clean and mildew-free longer by wiping down the shower and bathtub with a chamois cloth after each shower. The chamois cloth also works well on stainless-steel fixtures and sinks.

Bloodstains

Eradicate fresh bloodstains from fabric with salt, which breaks down red blood cells.

If you prick your finger while sewing and a drop or two of blood gets on the material, simply spit on a tissue and rub it over the stain.

Brass

To clean brass fixtures quickly and easily, apply a mix of equal parts vinegar and ketchup. Buff with a clean terry-cloth towel.

Polish tarnished brass by sprinkling it with baking soda. Take half a lemon and squeeze the juice over the baking soda, then scrub with the lemon. You'll find that the baking soda fizzes the tarnish off the brass.

Bric-a-Brac

If you have a house filled with glass or ceramic bric-a-brac, wash all the pieces that are not extremely delicate in your dishwasher—normal cycle—and your treasures will come out sparkling clean.

Here's a great way to dust a collection of small items without lifting each piece: Blow off the dust with a hair dryer turned on the lowest setting.

Butcher Block

Clean and disinfect the surface of butcher block by wiping with a solution of 1 part bleach and 10 parts water. Don't let the water sit on the surface and don't submerge a board in the solution for more than a moment. The wood could swell or split.

If a butcher block surface is deeply scarred from cutting, sand it with fine sandpaper until it is smoother. Deep crevices in the wood can harbor hard-to-eradicate germs.

Squeeze a bit of lemon juice on butcher block to eliminate odors.

Keep the wood conditioned by rubbing in mineral oil generously with a soft cloth when the butcher block is dry. Allow the oil to soak in for at least half an hour before wiping the surface down. Never use vegetable oil or animal fat, which can turn rancid.

C

Candles and Candle Wax

Restore shine to decorative candles by wiping them down with a cotton ball dipped in alcohol.

To make it easier to remove candle stubs from your fancy candlesticks, put a teaspoon of water or a small amount of petroleum jelly on the bottom of the holder before placing the candle inside.

● Candle wax drip on your carpet? Try this: Put a brown paper bag over the spot, then press with a warm (not hot!) iron. Continue to iron with fresh paper until all of the stain is absorbed.

● Can't get the candle wax out of that heirloom candelabra? Use a hair dryer to melt the wax and then pour it out into a garbage bag.

● To remove candle wax from glass votives, put them in the freezer for a few hours—the wax will pop right out.

Carpets

● Make unsightly footprints disappear from carpets. Spray the area with shaving cream, then vacuum. (First, test a small corner of your carpet for colorfastness.)

● Clean carpet stains with a mix of laundry detergent, water, and white vinegar.

● Tar deposits on your carpet? Loosen the tar with nonbutane lighter fluid, then follow up with a heavy-duty cleaner.

● If you're steam-cleaning your carpets—or having them professionally cleaned—protect

furniture legs from cleaning solution by "dressing" the legs in cotton sports socks secured with rubber bands. This also keeps furniture stain from bleeding onto the damp rug.

● Scatter some baking soda on carpets before you start your cleaning routine. By the time you get around to vacuuming, the baking soda will have absorbed some odors. An added bonus: You'll also be able to see exactly where you vacuumed—and where you didn't—by the telltale white powder.

Chalkboards

● Sprinkle baking soda on a damp rag and wipe the surface.

An upside-down umbrella makes a nifty drip catcher.

Chandeliers

● Chandeliers are usually quite difficult to clean. But for a sparkling clean chandelier the easy way, use a cloth and a solution of two parts rubbing alcohol and one part warm water. Don't forget this trick too: Hang an umbrella upside down from the chandelier to catch the drips.

Chrome

● To polish chrome, wet the metal and use the shiny side of a

5 Must-Have Cleaning Tools

These items help minimize cleaning time and maximize results.

Chamois Cloth

Available at most hardware stores and home improvement centers, this soft cloth is lint-free and highly absorbent. Its extra absorbency makes it ideal to use in a bathroom to wipe down tile and fixtures. The extra-soft fabric is gentle on all kinds of furniture, and because it's lint-free, it's especially good for cleaning windows and mirrors. Keep several in the house and use the same cloth for specific surfaces—one for glass, one for wood, one for tile. You don't want to mix up the rags and risk putting the wrong cleanser or polish on a surface.

Cotton String Mop

While a sponge mop is easy to use, it often pushes dirt and grime into corners instead of picking it up. A cotton string mop is a house cleaner's best bet for safely swabbing all solid-surface flooring—tile, wood, vinyl. Keep it clean by soaking it in a solution of bleach and hot water, rinsing with water and a half capful of fabric softener, then standing it, mop side up, outside to dry.

Rubber Gloves

Protect your hands from harsh chemicals and bacteria by wearing rubber gloves. They also allow you to use extra-hot water to help speed cleanup time. Keep a set in the kitchen, a set in the bathroom, and a set with your cleaning supplies so you never have any excuse not to wear them. Then treat yourself to a manicure when the cleaning's done.

Scrubber Sponge

Use a scrubber sponge to save yourself the extra step of scrubbing with a brush and then washing and rinsing with a sponge. Keep a separate sponge for each cleanser. (Attach the sponge to the cleanser with a rubber band so you won't mix up sponges and chemicals.) To keep sponges clean and smelling fresh, see *Sponges,* page 133.

Squeegee

Popular as a car windshield-cleaning device, this is one tool that you'll learn to love having around the house. Keep one in each bathroom and use it to wipe down tile walls and glass doors after every shower to prevent soap scum buildup and mildew from forming. When it's window-washing time, a spray with a nonstreaking cleaning solution (see *Windows,* page 136) and then a quick swipe with a squeegee will cut cleaning time in half.

---

piece of aluminum foil to rub the chrome. The foil will turn black, but the chrome will shine like new. Another option: Scrub chrome fixtures with dry baking soda or flour.

● Rubbing alcohol on a soft cloth removes drips and grease from chrome fixtures. Dry thoroughly after cleaning.

Clean Routine

● Straighten up and put things away the day *before* you clean. A clutter-free room is easier to clean.

● Give yourself a time limit for cleaning—even set a timer in your house for the allotted hours. It's a ploy, but you'll move faster if you know you're on the clock.

● Don't stop to answer the phone or look through papers. Also, keep the television turned off so you won't be tempted to stop and watch.

● Always clean one room completely before moving on to the next one. Move in a clockwise direction—avoid crisscrossing—toward the door.

● Put gravity to good use: Clean from top to bottom. Use a dust mop on ceilings first, then walls, furniture, and finally, floors.

● Put time on your side: For items that need to soak, or cleanser that needs to sit (oven cleaner, for example), get them going before you start to clean. By the time you finish the rest of the house, those items will be ready to be rinsed or wiped down.

● When scrubbing, work in all four directions: up, down, back, and forth.

Cleaning Supplies

● Save money on cleaning supplies by purchasing them from a janitorial supply company (listed in the Yellow Pages). Not only will you be able to buy generic cleaning solutions at less cost than supermarket brands, but you'll also find cleaning tools you won't necessarily find in your local hardware store or supermarket.

● A wallpaper soaking tray— long and rectangular in shape—makes an ideal "bucket" for a large sponge mop. The mop head fits completely into the tray with room to spare, which prevents splashing on the floor. You can buy these inexpensive plastic trays at hardware, wallpaper, and paint supply stores.

● Place heavy-duty floor mats—not decorative ones—at each entrance to your home to reduce the amount of dirt and grime being tracked inside. Encourage family members to remove shoes at the door too.

Coffee Stains

● To remove coffee stains in cups or on countertops, try a little baking soda instead of your usual cleanser. It works well and won't leave any gritty residue.

Computers

● If you eat while you work at your computer (and we all do occasionally), crumbs may fall into the keyboard. To clean it, disconnect the keyboard from the computer, turn it upside down, and hit the back of the keyboard with the flat of your hand to dislodge debris. A can of compressed air will blow out built-up dust.

● Wipe down sticky keys with baby wipes. Or dip a cotton swab in rubbing alcohol and clean each key.

● Clean the monitor with used dryer fabric-softener sheets dipped in alcohol. Not only will this leave the screen streak-free, but it will also leave behind an antistatic residue that will discourage dust from sticking to the surface.

Cookware

● Here's a quick and easy way to clean nonstick cookware: Mix 2 cups water and ½ cup dish detergent. Pour the solution into the pot or pan that needs cleaning and let the liquid sit for 5 minutes. Wash the cookware thoroughly with warm water, then dry with a cloth.

Curtains

● To remove dust from curtains, take them down and put a few panels in

5 Everyday Items That Can Clean Your Whole House

Before you stock up on commercial cleansers, consider using these.

Baking Soda (Sodium Bicarbonate)

An alkali, baking soda can soften hard water to eliminate hard-water spots and enhance the cleansing action of laundry soap. It can be dissolved in water to create a deodorizing solution or mixed with just a little water to make a gentle cleansing abrasive. Because it is an alkali, baking soda tends to darken aluminum, so rinse thoroughly after cleaning aluminum pots and surfaces with it.

Lemon Juice

Mildly acidic, lemon juice can be used to remove rust stains from porcelain sinks and tubs without causing any damage to the surface. When mixed with warm water, it helps cut through filmy residue on glass, mirrors, and dishes without leaving spots.

Household Bleach

An alkali, common household bleach is an excellent disinfectant. Mix it with warm water to wipe down tub and toilet. For a highly effective antimildew agent, mix a solution of ¾ cup bleach and 1 gallon water, then fill a spray bottle with it. Just spray on bathroom tile and grout, let sit for 5 minutes, then wipe down with a scrubber sponge. For tougher mildew on grout, scrub with a toothbrush. Keep a spray bottle of the solution in the kitchen to disinfect food prep surfaces and keep bacteria at bay.

Cream of Tartar

A powder commonly used in baking, cream of tartar can be mixed with water and used to brighten aluminum ware. It is also useful as a cleanser for aluminum and stainless steel, particularly coffeepots, because it neutralizes acidity and "sweetens" the pot. Mixed with a bit of lemon juice to form a paste, it makes a mildly abrasive cleanser for tougher stains.

Distilled White Vinegar

Also mildly acidic, distilled white vinegar can be added to dishwater to cut through grease. When mixed with warm water, it's an excellent nonstreaking solution for tile floors and glass surfaces. It's also an effective rinse for removing soapy film from countertops, woodwork, and stovetops.

---

your dryer with half a fabric-softener sheet. Run the dryer on air-dry for 20 minutes. Rehang immediately so there's no need to iron.

● Even quicker: Vacuum curtains with the upholstery attachment. Work from top to bottom.

D

Decking

● With a stiff broom, scrub mildew from a wood deck with a solution of one part bleach and three parts water.

● To zap sap stains from a wood deck that has not been sealed, rub the spots with mineral spirits.

Dishes

● If you are moving to a new home, use paper towels instead of newspaper to wrap dishes, glasses, and other breakables. No black newsprint to wash off, and the towels can be recycled for cleanup jobs when you unpack.

● To clean dishes, fill the sink or a basin with water and add a tablespoon of baking soda. It softens hands, cuts through grease, and eliminates odors.

Dishrags

● Anchor dishrags beneath a glass on the top rack of the dishwasher to clean and disinfect them.

Dishwasher

● If your dishwasher smells stale and musty, try this: Load the bottom tray with clean dishes. Set a small bowl with ½ cup vinegar on the bottom tray. Run the dishes through a normal cycle. Do this only once or twice a year, as vinegar may corrode pipes.

● To clean out your dishwasher, run a regular cycle with Tang (instant orange drink) in the soap dispenser. It's the citric acid that does the trick.

Drains

● To prevent hard-water clogs from stopping up your drains, pour about ½ cup of equal parts white vinegar and boiling water down the kitchen, bathroom, and bathtub drains.

● Use a crochet hook to clean the hair particles from the drain of a clogged-up bathtub or sink.

Draperies

● Draperies looking creased rather than gently pleated or gathered? Hold a steamer in front of them and shake the fabric to revive it—but to avoid accidental water stains, first cover the steamer nozzle with a sweat sock to absorb any drips or spits.

Save old socks to wear as "dust mitts." You'll cover twice as much surface in half the time.

Dusting

● Sometimes it's difficult to get at the dust that settles in furniture's fine grooves and crevices. Instead of using a cloth, try a 2-inch soft-bristled paintbrush. It's also great for cleaning between piano keys and around the buttons on your TV, stereo, and VCR.

● A child-size shovel makes a perfect dustpan. It holds more debris than a regular dustpan, and the longer handle means less backbreaking bending.

● Want to finish your dusting duties in half the time? Wear old mismatched socks on each hand when you dust. Spray the socks with a bit of water or furniture polish and get busy with both hands.

● A lamb's wool mitt (available at hardware and floor-cleaning supply stores) is an excellent housecleaning tool. The mitt attracts dust like a magnet, is machine washable, and can be air-dried.

● Never dust with a terry-cloth towel. It leaves lint behind. Avoid using feather dusters as well. These just scatter the dust elsewhere. If you have very delicate items with intricate carvings or crevices where dust collects, use a soft-bristled paintbrush instead of a cloth.

● To prevent dust from forming on surfaces that are prone to static electricity (TVs or the top of the refrigerator, for example), wipe the surface down with a solution of one part liquid fabric softener and four parts water. For louvered doors and blinds, dip a cotton-gloved hand in this solution and wipe over the surface.

Gooey egg mess? Table salt makes it easy to wipe up.

● If you can't get to the "dust bunnies" under your fridge or washer, try this: With a rubber band, attach an old sock to the end of a yardstick and push the stick under the appliance. Works like a charm.

● Dust will stay on your dustpan—and not scatter back on the floor—if you dampen it slightly before using it. To make your dustpan easier to clean, apply furniture wax to it.

● Can't move heavy objects to dust underneath? Bring your leaf blower inside and blow the dust out so you can vacuum it up from another part of the room.

● Cathedral ceilings can also present a dusting challenge, but this clever idea should do the trick: Cover a helium balloon with a soft cloth. Attach an ultra-long string to the balloon so you can float it to the ceiling but still hold it in your hand as you walk around the room. Now guide the balloon into those hard-to-reach spaces.

E

Egg Spills

● Pour table salt on top of a broken egg to absorb the mess, then wipe.

Eyeglasses

● Rubbing alcohol is an excellent eyeglass cleaner. Applied with a paper towel, the alcohol dries almost instantly and keeps your lenses streak- and fog-free.

● Wet your lenses with premoistened disposable baby washcloths, then dry them with a soft clean cloth. Your glasses will sparkle.

F

Fabrics

● Grandma knew best when it came to cleaning stained fabrics. Old-fashioned yellow bar laundry soap zaps most stains—blood, salad oil, grass, and fruit juice usually disappear. Keep a bar by your washing machine. Just dampen the stain and rub with the soap, then wash the item as usual. Bonus: The soap won't damage washable silks.

● See *Clothes Care 101,* pages 153–163, for all sorts of helpful laundry tips, as well as a thorough stain removal chart.

Fans

● Spray furniture polish on the blades of your ceiling fan, then wipe. The polish gives the blades a nice sheen— and makes dusting a breeze too.

Faux Flowers

● To remove dust from delicate silk flowers, place the flowers in a brown paper bag half filled with uncooked rice. Close the bag and shake well. The flowers will come out dust-free.

● Or take silk flower arrangements outside and blow off dust with a hair dryer on the low or gentle setting.

Furniture polish on fan blades makes dusting a breeze

Fireplace

● To remove ash buildup on fireplace doors, use a solution of water and leftover ashes.

● You can also use oven cleaner on fireplace doors. Spray the cleaner on the glass, let it sit for about 20 minutes, then wipe clean. Remember to place a protective covering on carpet and flooring before spraying the doors.

Fish Tank

● The next time you clean out the fish bowl or tank, don't discard the old water and the dregs from the bottom of the tank. Instead, use them to water and feed your houseplants.

G
Garbage

● Use empty cardboard milk cartons to collect vegetable peelings, eggshells, and other small garbage scraps. Fold over the top to keep odors from escaping. When the carton is full, toss in the trash.

● To keep food scrap garbage from stinking up your garbage pails— especially in hot weather—use milk cartons or plastic grocery bags as containers and store them in your freezer until garbage pick-up day. (This also helps to keep raccoons and similar pests away from outdoor garbage pails.)

● Always have disposable garbage bags at the ready—stow them in the bottom of the garbage pail. When one bag is removed, another is ready to take its place.

● Make it easier to slide full disposable trash bags out of your garbage pail. Spray the inside of the pail with silicone spray.

● Eliminate odor from a smelly garbage pail by pouring a layer of cat litter on the bottom.

Glass

● To prevent lint buildup on any glass surface, add a capful of liquid fabric softener to a bucket of warm water, then use it to clean the glass.

Glassware

● If you're plagued by spots on your glassware after it's already gone through a cycle in the dishwasher, try this: Mix equal parts water, vinegar, and lemon juice in a spray bottle and spray the glasses before putting them in the washer.

● To put the shine back on your glass coffeepot or teapot, wipe the interior with a sponge dipped into a mixture of lemon juice and salt, then put some ice cubes into the pot and swish them around. Rinse thoroughly with water.

Grease Stains

● Here's how to clean up a messy, grimy grease or oil stain quickly and easily: Sprinkle the surface of the stain with some cornstarch to absorb most of the grease. Let it sit for a few minutes, then wipe with dry paper towels before finishing up with soapy water or a commercial cleaner. This works well on fresh oil stains on fabric, as well as on hard surfaces.

Grout

● Clean mildew from grout with a solution of one part bleach and four parts water. Rinse thoroughly, then dry. For hard-to-remove mildew, scrub with a toothbrush.

Gum on a rug? Ice gets you out of this sticky situation with ease.

Gum

● To remove chewing gum from a wood or glass surface, lubricate the gum with peanut butter and gently pull it off.

● If chewing gum gets stuck to your upholstered furniture, area rug, or clothing, place an ice cube or ice pack on top of the gum. When it hardens, carefully pick off the brittle pieces.

Clean hairball-soiled carpets by working rubbing alcohol into the stain.

H

Hair

● Dog and cat hair on the carpet? Spray a mixture of one part fabric softener and three parts water on your rug, wait a minute or two, then vacuum.

Hair Brushes and Combs

● Soak brushes and combs in warm water and baby shampoo (baking soda dissolved in warm water works too). Add a small amount of hair conditioner to the rinse water to help prevent static.

Hairballs

● If you have a cat, chances are you've had to clean up a hairball mess from your carpet at least once. The best way to remove the stain: Blot the mess, then saturate a cloth with rubbing alcohol and rub it into the stain. (Brush your cat frequently to prevent future hairball mishaps!)

Heel Marks

● Rub floors and furniture gently with a pencil eraser to remove rubber heel marks. Or wipe with a soft cloth dampened with rubbing alcohol.

Humidifier

● Once a week, add a tablespoon of bleach to the water in your humidifier. Let the machine run for a few hours while you're out of the room. This will keep the machine from smelling damp and musty.

I

Ink Spots

● A little rubbing alcohol on a rag will remove felt-tip ink stains from kitchen countertops.

● Hair spray removes ink from most fabrics. (See *Stain-Removal Chart,* pages 160–162.)

J
Jar Drips

● Before placing an opened jar of honey or jam on your pantry or kitchen cabinet shelf, place a paper cupcake liner under the jar to catch any drips. Replace the cupcake liner as needed. Use this idea for bottles of oil or syrup too.

K
Kitchen

● Place a bathroom rug in front of your kitchen sink to protect this high-traffic area of your kitchen floor. The rug will stay put because it's nonskid, and it can be washed in your machine.

> **A nonskid bathroom rug stays put— perfect for use in a kitchen.**

● Looking for a quick way to clean kitchen and bathroom faucets? Wipe them down with a cotton ball soaked in rubbing alcohol.

● Steel-wool pads will scour better and won't rust if you store them in the freezer rather than under your kitchen sink.

L
Labels

● To remove labels, use a hair dryer to soften the adhesive. Pull back a corner of the label, heat, and peel.

Laminate Surfaces

Here are several ways to spiff up soiled or tired laminate countertops or cabinets.

● Use a paste made of equal parts lemon juice (from a fresh lemon only) and baking soda to remove old grease stains. Rinse very well.

● To revitalize dull-looking laminates, spray some furniture polish on the surfaces after you have scrubbed them clean. Rub with a soft cloth to make them shine.

● Try a nonabrasive all-purpose cleanser or a solution of liquid dishwashing detergent and water on a sponge or soft cloth. Rinse with a clean soft cloth wrung with water.

● Remove stubborn stains with a paste of baking soda and water applied with a soft cloth.

● For extremely tough stains, wipe with a cloth moistened with bleach.

● To restore shine to a dull-looking laminate countertop, use a specially formulated cleaner or cleaner-wax.

Lampshades

● Lampshades looking a little dusty? Use a dryer fabric-softener sheet instead of a cloth to wipe off lampshades. Not only does it remove existing dust, but it also prevents the buildup of static electricity, reducing the amount of dust attracted to the shade.

M
Marble

● Wipe up spills and spots immediately. Apply a nonabrasive cleanser; rub with a sponge or cloth. Rinse with clean water and dry with a clean soft cloth. Do not use acid-type cleansers, which can cause pitting.

FOOD AND BEVERAGE STAINS

● Make a paste of hydrogen peroxide (hair-bleaching strength) and whiting (an abrasive powder available at hardware stores). Add a few drops of clear household ammonia. Spread the paste on the stained area of marble, cover with plastic wrap, and let stand several hours. Repeat as necessary.

Rinse with water; dry thoroughly with a clean soft cloth.

BUTTER AND OIL STAINS

● Wipe the marble surface with an ammonia-dampened cloth. Make a paste of amyl acetate (available at drugstores), acetone, ammonia, and whiting. Spread on stains, cover with plastic wrap, and let stand for several hours. Repeat as needed. Rinse with water and dry with a clean soft cloth.

Mattresses

● On the first day of each season, flip mattresses over and rotate from head to toe to prevent lumps and sagging spots from forming in them.

Flip your mattress at the start of each season.

● To freshen up a mattress that hasn't been used in a while (in a vacation house or guest room, for example), sprinkle with baking soda or borax and let it sit overnight. Vacuum the next day. You can also sprinkle some baking soda between the mattress and the box springs or platform.

● If the mattress is really old and smells musty, sprinkle cat litter on top and allow it to sit for a week before vacuuming up.

Microwave Ovens

● Here's a fast and easy way to clean your microwave oven: Microwave 2 cups water on high for 2 minutes and let the water sit in the oven with the door closed for 5 minutes. Wipe the microwave clean with a sponge. Add a bit of lemon juice or vanilla to the water to leave behind a fresh scent.

Miniblinds

● To clean nonfabric miniblinds, fill the bathtub with hot water, add a squirt or two of dishwashing liquid, and let the blinds soak for 15 minutes. Then rinse them under the shower. Hang the blinds on the shower curtain rod or over the door to dry.

● For vinyl blinds, try this outdoor method: Simply lay the blinds in your driveway and spray them with a foaming cleanser. Rinse thoroughly with a hose, then hang the blinds on a clothesline to dry.

● Use a damp dryer fabric-softener sheet to quick-clean miniblinds and reduce the static cling that attracts dust.

● Degrease kitchen miniblinds by spraying with foaming bathroom cleanser. Close the blinds first, then spray a few slats at a time. Wipe thoroughly with a clean cloth dipped in hot water.

Mirrors

● A bit of rubbing alcohol on a soft lint-free cloth is great for cleaning mirrors (as well as windows). You won't have streaks, and the glass stays cleaner longer.

N
Nail Polish

● Use shaving cream and a clean cloth to blot spilled nail polish off furniture or floors. Rinse off the cream, then dry the surface thoroughly.

Nonstick Pans

● If a nonstick pan doesn't just wipe clean, fill it with water, heat to simmering, and rub the soiled area gently with a wooden or plastic spatula.

O
Odors

● Here's an inexpensive way to deodorize a garbage disposal: Make ice cubes with water and ½ cup white vinegar; put them in the disposal and turn it on. The cubes deodorize the disposal and also sharpen the blades.

● Place a few lemon wedges in the freezer to eliminate freezer odor. Replace them as needed.

● If a foul odor, like spoiled or bad fish, has taken over your kitchen, try this trick: Place a bowl of white vinegar on the counter and let it sit for a few hours. Before you know it, the odor will have disappeared and the room will smell fresh again.

● Clear a room of the smell of cigarette, cigar, or pipe smoke by dipping a small hand towel into a solution of equal parts vinegar and hot water. Wring out the towel and then gently wave it around the room. The smell should clear within minutes.

● To remove food odors that linger in your microwave, put 3 or 4 lemon slices in a bowl, add ¾ cup water, and bring to a boil (about 3 minutes) in your microwave. Leave the bowl in the microwave for 10 minutes, then clean

the inside with a sponge and the lemony water.

● Get rid of musty odor in an old book: Put one half of a dryer fabric-softener sheet in the book's front cover, the other half inside the back.

● To fill your home with the smell of citrus, throw a handful of orange peels into a pot of boiling water.

● Eliminate stale, musty odors in a basement or garage. Fill a net vegetable bag (the kind onions come in) with pieces of charcoal and hang it in a corner of the room.

● If you can't get to the laundry for a day or two, fill a sock or an old nylon knee-high with baking soda, tie off the end, and toss it in the hamper with the dirty clothes to keep the hamper smelling sweet.

● If you've got a wooden canister that's taken on an unpleasant odor, fill it with coffee grounds and then let it sit, sealed, for a few days.

● Stuff smelly sneakers with newspaper to remove odor.

Wave a vinegar-soaked towel around a room to remove smoke odor.

Oven

● Here's a no-fuss way to clean a conventional oven: Place ½ cup ammonia in a small bowl and leave it uncovered in the cold oven overnight. The ammonia fumes will loosen any baked-on residue. In the morning, add water to the ammonia, dampen a sponge, and use the solution to clean the oven door, walls, and racks.

● Clean the range hood filter in your dishwasher.

● Do you have a self-cleaning oven? Before you turn it on, toss in a few whole cloves and cinnamon sticks. You'll have a clean oven and a house that smells like freshly baked cakes and cookies.

P

Pet Dining Area

● Place your pet's food and water dishes on top of an old rubber bathtub mat. The mat's suction cups keep it from sliding, and the rubber is easy to wipe clean.

Plastic Containers

● Tea or tomato stains making your plastic containers look less than appetizing? Mix a bit of bleach with lots of hot water inside the container. Let it stand for 5 minutes, then rinse.

Plastic Furniture

● The bright colors of outdoor plastic furniture and kiddie gyms can fade from regular exposure to the sun. Applying a protective coat of car wax

not only prevents them from fading but also repels dirt and grime, which makes for quick and easy cleanups.

Plastic Shower Curtain

● You can clean your shower curtain in the washing machine using the "Delicate" cycle and warm water. Add bleach and liquid fabric softener (to keep the curtain soft). Do not allow the curtain to go through the spin cycle. Hang it in the bathroom or outdoors on a clothesline to dry.

Plush Toys

● If your child's toys are fully machine washable, follow the directions on the label. To clean nonwashable plush toys, put them inside a pillowcase or lingerie bag, place in the dryer, and tumble on "Air Dry" or "Fluff Only" to remove dust.

Porcelain

● To get rid of stains in your porcelain teapot, place a denture-cleaning tablet in the pot, fill it with water, and let it sit overnight. Wash as usual.

● Do you like to make fresh berry pies and jams but hate the stains the fruit leaves on your porcelain sink? Next time, fill the sink with warm water and add a denture-cleaning tablet to the water. The solution will remove stains from the sink, bowls, and utensils.

Pots and Pans

● If the bottoms of your pots and pans are discolored or burned, rub them spotless by using a paste of two parts salt and one part white vinegar on a wet sponge.

● Do you have an aluminum pot that's discolored from a chemical reaction (contact with an acid like tomato sauce, for example)? To make it shiny again, just fill the pot with water and add 3 tablespoons cream of tartar. Simmer until the discoloration disappears. Bonus: The cream of tartar "sweetens" the pot for a less bitter-tasting sauce next time.

● Spray the bottoms of badly discolored or burned pots with oven cleaner, set them upside down on an empty trash bag or old newspaper, and leave overnight. Wipe clean with a damp sponge and rinse well.

● Here's some food for thought: To shine a stainless-steel pot, fill it with 3 cups tomato juice and bring to a boil, then wash and dry the pot as usual.

Polish aluminum pots with cream of tartar. Tomato juice works on stainless steel.

● Use dishwasher crystals to remove baked- or burned-on food from pots and pans. Place some crystals in the dirty pot or pan, add hot water, and let the item soak for an hour. Sponge off the food and rinse thoroughly.

Q
Quilts

● To keep quilts—old and new—from discoloring or fading in storage, roll and store them (after cleaning) in acid-free paper, available in art supply stores.

● If you can't find acid-free paper, wrap quilts in clean white cotton sheets or washed unbleached muslin.

● To clean fragile quilts, vacuum them gently—place a stocking over the vacuum brush attachment first.

R
Radiators

● Use a bottle brush—the long narrow kind—to clean radiator crevices. Soak the brush in soapy water first, then scrub the radiator.

Rust

● Are there rust rings on your countertop? Put a thick paste made of lemon juice and a bit of salt on the stains. After the paste dries, rinse with cool water.

● Remove rust from metal patio furniture with a bit of turpentine and elbow grease.

● To remove rust stains from your sink or bathtub, pour hydrogen peroxide and a sprinkle of cream of tartar on the rust. Let sit for 30 minutes, then clean with a sponge. Repeat the application if necessary.

S
Safety Devices

● Remember: The beginning of each season is a good time to make sure all your household safety devices, like smoke alarms, fire extinguishers, and carbon monoxide detectors, are in perfect working order. Replace the batteries, check the pressure gauges, and go over the entire fire drill plan with your family. (If you have an alarm system, this is a good time to be sure everyone knows how to use the fire and ambulance call features.)

Screens

● To remove debris from dirty screens, take them down and lay them on a plastic dropcloth outdoors. Scrub them with a brush and an all-purpose cleanser, and then hose them down.

Shutters

● Do not clean interior wood shutters or blinds with water, which can cause the wood to warp. Instead, use a soft chamois cloth treated with furniture polish.

Sponges

● Throw all of your grungy old kitchen sponges into the washing machine with a bleach load, let them dry, and then set them aside to use for cleaning the bathroom tub and tiles. They're great for washing the car too.
● To clean and refresh kitchen sponges, put them in the top rack of your dishwasher the next time you're ready to run a load of dishes.

● If your kitchen sponge smells sour, soak it in lemon juice, then rinse.

Stainless-Steel Sinks

● Do hard-water spots on your stainless-steel sink seem almost impossible to remove? Wipe them away with a sponge soaked in a mixture of 3 teaspoons laundry detergent and 1 cup warm water. Another option: Wipe down with a cloth dampened with white vinegar. Wipe dry quickly to prevent additional spotting.

T
Teapots

● To clean a tea-stained teapot, fill it with water and add ¼ cup bleach. Wash and rinse the pot thoroughly.
● To remove hard-water and lime buildup from a teakettle, pour in 2 cups white vinegar and bring to a boil. Let it simmer for about 10 minutes, then rinse well. The minerals will flake off.
● Place an agate marble in your teakettle, and you'll never have to clean out lime deposits again.

Telephone

● To clean and disinfect the receiver, wipe it with rubbing alcohol.
● Does your cordless phone have trouble staying charged? Examine the metal contacts on both the receiver and the base unit. If they look dull or have dirt buildup, try this: Use a pencil eraser to gently rub off the grime. Cleaner contacts enable the phone to recharge fully.

Television

- Never spray any cleanser on a television set—the solution may end up where it shouldn't and cause a short.
- To clean the screen, wipe it down with a dryer fabric-softener sheet dipped in rubbing alcohol. This also will help to repel dust.
- Use mild soap and water on a cloth to wipe down the exterior. Or if your TV set is in a wood cabinet, clean with a product made specifically for wood, such as Murphy's Oil Soap.

Textiles

- Always follow the manufacturers' labels to clean household textiles. See *Clothes Care 101,* pages 153–163, for all sorts of helpful laundry tips, as well as a thorough stain-removal chart.

Thermos

- To remove tough coffee stains from a thermos, fill it with ice, water, and some table salt. Shake well, then wash.
- Try this quick and inexpensive thermos cleaning trick: Dissolve 2 tablespoons ordinary baking soda in ½ cup boiling water and use the mixture to clean and deodorize a bottle that is badly stained, has been in storage for a long time, or was left, uncleaned, in a school or gym locker.

Toothbrushes

- Put your toothbrushes in the dishwasher once a month or so to disinfect them. Also run them through after you or others in your house have had colds.

To perk up a moldy patio umbrella, spray it with mildew remover, then hose off.

U
Umbrella

- Spray a moldy patio umbrella with a mildew remover. Let stand for about 10 minutes, then hose it down. Allow it to dry before closing.

Upholstery

- Looking for a quick and easy way to remove lint and pet hair from upholstery and car seats? Wear a latex glove and simply wipe your hand across the material. The hair will stick to the glove like glue.
- If your good upholstered furniture becomes seriously stained, be smart. Have a professional service clean it rather than risk making the damage worse with a home remedy. Look in the Yellow Pages or ask your local dry cleaner for a referral.

V

Vacuuming

● To avoid lugging that heavy vacuum cleaner up and down the stairs so often, organize your routine so that you vacuum downstairs first, then work your way up. Next time, start with the upstairs rooms and work your way down.

● Or attach an extra-long extension cord—30 feet or longer—to your vacuum cleaner so you can move it all over the house without having to replug.

● A small handheld vacuum cleaner is ideal for stairs because you can clean both risers and steps easily. Remember to work from top to bottom.

● Vacuum the inside of a dresser drawer without emptying the contents. Simply cover the nozzle of the vacuum hose with panty hose first.

Varnish

● Soak a varnish stain on wood, tile, or vinyl with turpentine or paint thinner. Rinse with cool water. If this is not effective, repeat the process, but first rub the area with a bar of white hand soap.

Vases

● Remove stains from the inside or bottom of a vase by pouring tea leaves soaked in warm water inside. Shake the tea leaves around the vase, then pour them out. Rinse. You can also let a vase filled with cold tea or vinegar sit overnight.

● Lime deposits may cause a vase to become cloudy. If this happens, fill the vase with water and drop in a denture-cleaning tablet or two. You can also add a few dried beans or some uncooked rice to the cleaning solution. Stir them around so they'll clean the crevices. Dishwasher detergent in warm water may also do the trick. Swish it around and rinse thoroughly.

Vinyl Floors

● Scuff marks on vinyl floors come off quickly and easily with just a bit of liquid dishwashing detergent mixed with an equal amount of warm water. (Note: Rinse thoroughly if this solution is used on no-wax vinyl floors.)

Vomit Stains

● To remove a vomit stain from wool carpeting, pour club soda on the stain. On a nonwool rug, apply a mixture of 1 part ammonia and 10 parts water. Rinse with cold water, let the rug dry, then vacuum.

W

Walls

● Use small squares of leftover carpeting to clean heavily textured plaster walls. The thick pile cleans uneven surfaces without shredding but is soft enough not to damage walls.

● Never spray an aerosol cleanser (for vinyl window trim, for example) where it may stain an adjacent wall surface. Instead, spray the cleanser onto a soft cloth, then wipe it on.

● To clean heavily stained painted

walls, especially around light switches, apply a scouring solution of baking soda and water with a soft cloth.

Washable Wallpaper

● Use a solution of 2 tablespoons ammonia and 4 cups water to clean scuffs and handprints from wallpaper. If the wallpaper is scrubbable, you can apply the ammonia-water solution with a soft-bristled scrub brush. Work from top to bottom and rinse thoroughly.

Washing Machine

● Here's how to remove mineral deposits that build up in your washing machine: Once a month, fill the main tub of the washer with warm water and a cup of vinegar. Run the machine through an entire cycle. To preserve the outside, wax the machine with car wax twice a year.

● To remove fabric softener and bleach deposits from inside your washing machine, pour some hot water into the holder where you'd normally place the fabric softener or bleach, then run the machine. Works like magic.

The perfect lint-free cloth for windows: A remnant from old, worn jeans.

● Too many suds in your washing machine? The culprit is probably too much detergent. Don't panic: Pour in ½ cup salt or an average measure of liquid fabric softener to dissipate the suds.

Waxing Floors

● Here's a tip for those of you who use a cloth to wax floors: First, soak the cloth in cold water and wring it out. The cloth absorbs less wax, which means less waste.

Windows

● Windshield wiper fluid is great for cleaning windows, appliances, and no-wax floors—and it's less expensive than most conventional cleaning solutions.

● A rag cut from a pair of old, worn-out jeans makes a fine lint-free cloth for washing windows.

● If you want to avoid streaks (and who doesn't), don't clean your windows on a hot or sunny day. Cool and overcast is better.

Wine

● Hold a wine-stained tablecloth over a bowl and cover the stain with table salt. Pour boiling water over the salt until the stain disappears.

● To clean a delicate, narrow-necked wine decanter easily, place two antacid tablets and a handful of sand in the decanter. Add warm water, swish, and let sit for a minute or two.

Swish the mixture again, then rinse thoroughly.

Wood

● Wipe your (stained and sealed, not painted) baseboards, wood cabinets, and other wood fixtures with no-wax floor cleaner. They will shine like new.

Y

Yard Equipment

● Rub some liquid car wax on yard tools—lawn mower or snow blower, for example—to help keep them clean and rust-free. This also works well on metal swing sets and lawn furniture.

Yarn

● If you knit, here's a way to keep your yarn clean: Remove the black "dish" from the bottom of a clean 2-liter soda or water bottle. Cut off the clear bottom of the bottle and slip the ball of yarn inside, pulling a single strand through the neck opening at the top. Then replace the black "dish." The yarn stays neat, clean, and untangled.

● Keep a bunch of baby wipes in a resealable plastic bag and store them with your knitting or needlework. No matter where you are, you'll be able to clean your hands before working.

Z

Zinc Oxide

● A pigment often found in cosmetics and sunscreen, zinc oxide can leave a yellow stain on clothes. Pretreat the stain with a laundry product containing enzymes. Wash as usual.

Season-by-Season Home Maintenance Guide

Taking care of these regular chores each season can keep your home running smoothly.

SPRING

● Wash windows, clean screens, and remove storm windows.

● Check your roof for leaks: On a sunny day, stand in your yard and use binoculars to find damage. Repair or replace broken, bent, or missing tiles and shingles. On a rainy day, use a flashlight to see water drips in the attic.

● Replace washing-machine hoses annually to prevent leaks.

● Plan your garden, or if you live in warmer climates, plant your garden.

● Prep flower beds, window boxes, and other planters for bedding plants.

● Service and clean your lawn mower and garden tools.

● Check your home's exterior wood trim for damage. Look for cracks, blistering paint, warping, and soft places—which can mean dry rot. Make repairs as needed and touch up exterior paint.

● Uncover and check the condition of air conditioners, lawn mower, lawn furniture, outdoor lightbulbs, outdoor grill, swing set and slides, outdoor faucets, gutters, pools, and hot tubs.

● Test fire extinguishers and alarms.

● Clean chandeliers and other light fixtures, lamps, and lampshades.

● Launder or dry-clean curtains and drapes; clean blinds.

● Flip mattresses; vacuum behind and under bed.

SUMMER

● Scrub your barbecue grill with a wire brush and oven cleaner (wear rubber gloves).

● Clean your patio furniture and repair as needed.

● Make sure all windows in your home open smoothly. If not, paint a thin coat of petroleum jelly on the tracks or run a pizza cutter back and forth in the grooves that are sticking.

● Pressure-wash your home's exterior, driveway, and walkways. Check local equipment companies for rental rates.

● Give your automobile a good cleaning—inside and out.

● Flip and turn the cushions on furniture to help them wear evenly.

● Purge the linen closet. Keep two sets of linens for each bed in your house. Make rags from torn sheets.

FALL

● Winterize your lawn mower: Clean it, change the oil, and drain the gas.

● Stock up on firewood. Ensure you'll always have a dry supply by keeping wood in a large plastic garbage can at your back door.

● Replace heating system filters in your home and have the system professionally serviced if necessary.

● Clear out leaves and debris from gutters and downspouts.

● Vacuum the padding and the floor beneath all the rugs in your home. Turn area rugs around so they'll wear evenly. Do this at least twice a year.

● Insulate exposed water shutoffs outside your home.

● Lubricate the locks throughout your house: Rub a soft pencil (No. 1 or No. 2) on both sides of the matching key until it's well covered. Now insert and remove the key from the lock a few times. Do this again in the spring.

WINTER

● Close the chimney flue when the fireplace is not in use.

● Replace furnace filter.

● Set a goal to clean out all your closets and drawers. Tackle one closet and two drawers until you're done.

● Unscrew the aerator from the end of each faucet, wash carefully; replace.

● Vacuum coils beneath refrigerator to increase efficiency. Make a note to do this three more times during the year.

● Inspect ceramic tile around the tub or shower. Caulk as needed.

● Do an attic and basement safety check. Are paints or flammable liquids stored away from the furnace or hot-water heater? Make sure the circuit breaker box is well marked. Look for evidence of frayed wiring.

● Fix hairline cracks in interior walls with joint compound.

● Inspect outside of house for winter damage: Check walls, driveways, and garage floors for cracks or crumbling.

● Drain a gallon or so from the bottom of your hot-water heater to remove sediment.

At the end of this season:

● Clean and store winter equipment, such as shovels and snow blowers.

● Hose down or vacuum all of your outdoor entry mats.

● Wash and pack away winter clothes, coats, boots, and accessories.

Car Smarts

You probably spend so much time in your car, it starts to feel like home.

It's not *really* your home, but then, again, some days it probably feels like it. Since many of us rely on our cars so much—and spend so much time in them—it's important to keep them in tip-top condition, inside and out. But we also tell you what to stash in your trunk so you're prepared just in case you do have to deal with a breakdown.

Clean Machine

● If you take your car to a car wash, select only one that's brushless. The brushless wash is easier on the car's finish than a wash with spinning brushes.

● When washing your car at home, find a shady spot to park and allow the engine to cool before you begin. A warm car causes water and soap to spot as the car dries.

● Remove the mats from the car and set them on the driveway or another hard-surface area. Placing them on the grass can damage the turf.

● Let everyone in the family help wash the car—there's enough for everyone to do. For example, have little ones empty out the car debris: papers, pencils, juice boxes, and loose change. Make sure they check under the seats and mats, inside ashtrays and door handles. You can also give the youngsters rags, scrub brushes, and a bucket or dishpan full of warm soapy water and let them scrub the mats.

● Vacuum out the car. A small but powerful handheld vacuum is ideal for car interiors. This job is perfect for younger kids because they can crawl in and out of a car's tight spaces easily.

● Starting at the roof and working your way down, first hose your car off with gentle to moderate pressure in order to dislodge loose dirt and soften stuck-on debris. Don't forget the wheel wells.

● To wash the car, use a commercial car soap from an auto supply store, not dishwashing liquid or household detergent, which are too harsh and can damage the finish. Using a soft cloth, begin washing the roof and work your way down—one panel at a time—around the car.

● Use a back-and-forth motion as you work, rinsing the car often with clean water to remove sand and dirt that could scratch the car's surface. Older kids can clean the top part of the car; younger ones, the bottom part. Assign even younger children to wash headlights, taillights, and hubcaps.

● Using a mixture of baking soda and water, clean car lights, chrome, and enamel with a soft cloth. Don't use sponges for this; they carry dirt, which may scratch these surfaces.

Let little ones help when it's car cleanup time.

• Give the car a final rinse with the hose. Remove the nozzle and set the hose so a medium flow of water can cascade over the car. The sheeting action of the water will make the drying process easier.

• With a soft lamb's wool mitt or chamois cloth, dry the car from the top down. Don't forget to wipe off headlights, taillights, and hubcaps.

• Clean wiper blades with rubbing alcohol. Not only does this keep them clean, but it also discourages ice from forming on the blades.

Windows and Mirrors

• Use a commercial window-cleaning solution or window wash, or make your own solution of equal parts water and rubbing alcohol in a spray bottle. Don't use glass wax, which tends to leave a film layer of wax on the surface.

• First, wipe down windows to remove the dust, then spray on the window-cleaning solution and wipe off the windows with a lint-free cloth. Make sure not to perform this operation in the bright sun; windows will streak. Don't forget to wipe off the mirrors.

• Used dryer fabric-softener sheets make excellent lint-free window-washing and wiping cloths. And they leave behind a nice fresh scent.

• A new and unused chalk blackboard eraser is great for cleaning steamed-up car windows from within the car. Keep the eraser in a resealable plastic bag between cleanings and stow it in the glove compartment or console.

Sticky Solutions

• Tree sap is tough to remove from your car and, if left unchecked, can ruin the finish. Remove sticky sap with a soft cloth soaked in olive or other vegetable oil. Rub in a circular motion until you have removed the sap.

• WD-40, a commercial degreaser, is also good for removing sticky residue from a car's surface.

Renew whitewall tires by spraying with oven cleaner, then hosing off.

Tire Magic

• Whitewall tires look awful when they get dirty and scuffed. To clean them easily, remove the hubcaps and spray the tires with commercial oven cleaner. Let sit for a few minutes, then rinse with a hose. No scrubbing needed.

• To make chrome hubcaps look like new, polish them with a balled-up piece of aluminum foil, shiny side out.

• A commercial vinyl cleaner, like Armor All, can restore the shine to dull-looking whitewalls.

Caring for Your Car

WHAT TO CHECK	HOW TO DO IT	WHEN
Air filter	Unscrew nut holding metal lid to filter housing; remove lid and lift out filter. If only slightly dirty, tap on a hard surface to dislodge dirt. Replace filter when it's extremely dirty or as part of a tune-up.	Every month or two
Antifreeze/ coolant level	Newer cars have see-through reservoirs with level markings. Top off with a 50/50 solution of permanent antifreeze and water. Keep 1 inch below filler neck. Check with a cool engine, and never remove pressure cap when engine is hot.	Monthly or every 1,000 miles, whichever comes first; daily under heavy use
Battery and terminals	Make sure cables are attached securely and free of corrosion.	Monthly
Brake fluid	If you cannot check level without removing cover, wipe dirt from brake master cylinder reservoir lid. Pry off retainer clip and remove lid. If fluid is needed, add type approved for your car and check for possible leaks.	Monthly
Exhaust system	Look underneath car for broken or loose exhaust clamps or supports. Check for holes in muffler and pipes. Replace rusted or damaged parts.	Yearly; seasonally in high-salt areas
Fan belts and other drive belts	Check undersides of belts and replace worn, glazed, or frayed ones. Tighten them when they have more than ½ inch slack when depressed between pulleys. Replace bulging or rotten hoses and tighten clamps.	Monthly
Lights	Turn on and inspect headlights, brake lights, turn signals, and emergency flashers. Clean light covers whenever cleaning car.	Monthly
Oil	Remove dipstick, wipe it clean, insert it, and remove it again. If level marker indicates it's low, add oil. Drain and replace oil and change air filter every 3,000 miles or 3 months.	Every other gas fill-up

WHAT TO CHECK	HOW TO DO IT	WHEN
Power-steering fluid	Check when car is warm but not running by removing, wiping, and reinserting the reservoir dipstick. Fluid should be maintained between "Full" and "Add" markers.	Every 6 months or 6,000 miles, whichever comes first, or if you have steering problems
Tires	Keep inflated to recommended pressure; check with gauge when tires are cool. Inspect for cuts, bulges, excessive wear. Uneven wear indicates misalignment or out-of-balance tires.	Monthly; rotate every 5,000 to 10,000 miles
Transmission fluid	Engine should be warm and running, transmission in "Park," parking brake on. Remove dipstick, wipe dry, reinsert fully, and remove again. Do not mix fluid types and do not overfill.	Every 3,000 miles or 3 months, whichever comes first
Windshield wiper system	Replace blades before they become worn and brittle—at least once a year, more often if smearing or chattering occurs. Keep washer-fluid reservoir full; when topping off, use some solvent to clean wiper blades.	Monthly

Superior Interior

● To keep dashboards, vinyl interiors, and tires from dulling or cracking prematurely, use a silicone-based spray. Don't forget to wipe down the console, steering wheel, and—if you have a standard transmission—the clutch housing.

● Use commercial carpet-cleaning sprays to remove stains and spots from upholstered seats.

● Spray cleaned carpets and upholstery with commercial fabric protector. (Test first for colorfastness.) Fabric protector will keep your seats and carpets cleaner longer because spills won't penetrate the fabric. Reapply the fabric protector often.

● Apply a coat of liquid floor wax to rubber floor mats that have been washed. The wax finish will keep the mats new and will also make it easier to wipe off dirt and mud.

● No floor mats for your car? You can get inexpensive—often free—ones from your local carpet store. Just ask for old or outdated rug samples— they're the perfect size for a car's interior. You might even find ones that coordinate with the color of your car interior. Vacuum the rugs when necessary, and when they get old and worn, toss and replace them with new ones.

● Plastic grocery sacks with handles make terrific trash receptacles for the car. Hang them over the headrests of the front passenger and driver seats for back-seat passenger use. Hang another one in the front from the dashboard using a suction cup with a hook attachment.

● Put the last of the dishwashing liquid to good use. Fill the bottle with water and store it in your car with paper towels and a plastic bag. The mix is great for cleaning dirty hands, and the bag is handy for storing used paper towels.

● To absorb stale car odors, you can fill the ashtrays with baking soda.

● To keep your car smelling fresh— and to discourage smoking in your car—fill the ashtrays with potpourri. The heat from the car will release the scent of the potpourri.

● Tuck a dryer fabric-softener sheet in a few out-of-the-way spots in your car.

They'll give off a clean, fresh scent.
● Save empty square-shaped tissue boxes to use as trash receptacles for your car.

Wax On, Wax Off

● If waxing is recommended in the owner's manual, wax your car at least twice a year, once in the late spring, again in the late fall. Wax is not recommended for cars sheathed in plastic, but it keeps a metal car looking good and also protects the paint, prolonging the life of the finish.

● Use a product that cleans, polishes, and waxes in one step. Wash the car thoroughly first, however, so that you don't scratch the surface when you apply the cleaner.

● Pick a cool, overcast day to wax your car, or park it in a shady spot early or late in the day, before the heat

7 Ways to Prevent Car Theft

Take these steps to avoid becoming a victim.

1. Install one or more of the following preventive items: a top-quality alarm system; a hidden, secondary ignition switch; a jimmy-proof bar that locks on the steering wheel; a fuel shut-off device that will stop the car within seconds if not deactivated; an electronic device that tracks the car if it is stolen; an immobilizer that will disable the car's electrical system from up to a quarter mile if you see your car being stolen.

2. At home, park your car in the driveway, in a locked garage, or as close to your house as possible.

3. Always lock your car doors.

4. Never leave your car with the engine running or the key in the ignition.

5. In public areas, park as close to an open store or office as possible. Take note of where you are parked; forgetful and confused drivers are easy targets.

6. When you park in attended lots, leave the ignition key only. Some car models feature "valet" keys for this very purpose; they will only open car doors and fire the ignition.

7. At night, park in a lighted, well-frequented area. Get an escort if possible. Many shopping centers, large garages, and office complexes readily provide assistance to help you reach your car.

sets in. If the car is too hot or if the sun is beating down on the car, the wax will dry too quickly and be much more difficult to rub off.

● Use a lamb's wool mitt or chamois cloth when you wax. Apply wax to a small section of the car, allow it to set according to the manufacturer's directions, then wipe it off thoroughly with small circular motions.

Baby Car Seat Strategies

● Place an old bath towel or bedspread beneath the baby's car seat. When your youngster tosses food or a bottle onto the car seat, the towel or bedspread will protect the upholstery and can be tossed in the wash for easy cleanup.

A drop cloth under your baby's car seat can keep car mess to a minimum.

● Put insulating foam—the kind you buy for water and heating pipes—around the section of the metal frame that rests on the car's seat. The foam will protect the upholstery from rust stains and the deep depressions caused by the weight of the baby's car seat.

Battery Buying Smarts

● Don't wait until your car battery dies to replace it. The life expectancy of a battery is usually 4 or 5 years. A tired, weak battery makes it harder to

start the car and forces the alternator, the car's charging system, to burn out faster. Take your car to an automotive service center to have the battery tested. A fully charged battery should register 12.75 volts.

● Don't skimp on the size or cost of a new battery. Buy the biggest and longest-lasting battery that will fit into your car. Doing so will reduce some of the strain on your car's starting, charging, and electrical systems.

● Replace your old battery with a new one that has the same or greater CCA (cold-cranking amp) rating. This rating indicates the number of amps the battery can deliver for 30 seconds at 0 degrees Fahrenheit without going dead. (Be sure it says "Fahrenheit" next to the CCA rating, not "Celsius," which would signify a low temperature of only 32 degrees Fahrenheit. The battery would not be guaranteed to work at temperatures below that.)

All Charged Up

If your battery happens to go dead a year or so away from its warrantied life expectancy, check the following:

● Cable connections: Even if your battery has plenty of power, loose connections can prevent the energy from getting to the starter. Using a wrench, you can tighten the cable connections yourself.

● Dirty battery terminals: Terminals gunked up with grease and dirt can adversely affect your car's electrical systems, as well as its computer.

Trunk Show

● Store a plastic shower curtain or tablecloth in the trunk of your car. You can kneel on it when you have to change a tire or check for an oil leak. You can also spread it out to keep your trunk clean when you load in bags of soil or other messy items.

● If you have little ones, keep a spare box of diapers, some moist towelettes, baby powder, and a change of clothes in a travel bag in the trunk of your car. This system sure beats lugging a diaper bag around.

● In the trunk, also keep a suitcase or duffel bag filled with a change of old clothes—sweatpants, sweatshirt, hat, gloves, socks, sneakers, rain poncho. If you ever have to change a tire or walk a distance to find a gas station, you won't have to worry about ruining your dress clothes and shoes.

● Keep a roll of reflective tape in your trunk too. If a headlight or taillight burns out, place a piece of tape over it until you can get the bulb replaced. You can also stick the tape on your car or on its antenna if your car becomes disabled.

Driving Emergencies

Here's what to do if bad weather or mechanical failure catches you unaware:

HYDROPLANING

● Hydroplaning happens when water builds up in front of your tires faster than your car's weight is able to push it away. The car may feel as if it's gliding or out of control because the water gets between your tires and the road surface. (Worn tires are especially susceptible to this phenomenon.) If you think you're hydroplaning, resist the urge to slam on the brakes. Instead, take your foot off the gas pedal and let the car slow down naturally. By gradually allowing the tires and pavement to reconnect, this method prevents skidding.

If you're riding a wave of water on the road, don't slam on the brakes.

Low-beam lights are your best bet when driving through fog.

SKIDDING

● If your tires lose their grip on the road and start to spin, ease off the gas without stepping on the brake. Whether you are driving a rear-, front, or all-wheel-drive car, disengage the clutch or shift into neutral. *On rear-wheel-drive cars,* steer into the skid. This will allow the car to straighten out and stop skidding. Just before you come out of the skid, turn the wheel slightly until you are going in the direction you want to go. *On front-and all-wheel-drive cars,* steer in the direction of the skid until you feel the tires begin to grip, then use the brakes to regain control of speed before you steer in another direction. For all types, put the car back in gear and proceed.

NO TRACTION

● To stop a car in snow or ice with conventional brakes, reduce speed by "cadence braking"—step firmly on the brake until the wheels lock, then quickly release the brake, then repeat. For antilock brake systems (ABS), remember "stomp and steer." Step firmly on the brake and hold. You will probably feel the brake pedal vibrate or you may hear noises. The computerized system pumps the brakes faster than you can manually.

FOG

● Use your low-beam lights, not your brights, in dense fog. The moisture in the air reflects light back at you, making the low beams more effective. If your car has fog lights, you must have the low-beam light setting on before the fog lights can be activated.

DEAD BATTERY

● Never jump-start a disabled car when the ignition is on. In fact, the ignition in both the stalled car and the assisting vehicle should be turned off until all of the cables are connected. Attach one end of the red cable to the positive terminal (indicated by a +) of the live battery and the other end to the positive terminal of the dead battery. Clamp one end of the black cable to the negative (–) terminal of the live battery and the other end of the black cable to the negative terminal of the dead battery or to any other grounding point on the engine block of the stalled car. Start the assisting vehicle first, then the stalled car. Once the car is running, disconnect the cables in reverse order. Keep the revived car running for at least 30 minutes. Unless you are planning to drive continuously for several hours, have the battery professionally recharged.

If your car starts to overheat, open the windows and turn on the heat.

OVERHEATING

● Open all the windows in the car and turn on the heat full blast to draw heat away from the engine. When you're able to, pull into a gas station or rest area to allow the car to cool. Once the engine has cooled, carefully open the radiator cap, using a towel. *Keep your face away from the opening, in case steam or hot water escapes.* Pour water or antifreeze into the radiator. Check the oil and add more if necessary. Do not turn on the car's air conditioning or other extras until you determine the cause of the overheating.

DISABLED CAR

● If you can, get to the shoulder before your car dies completely. If you are forced to stop in the middle of the road, turn on the flashers and lift the engine hood to indicate that the car is disabled. If this unhappy incident occurs at night, light flares and place them around the car. Turn on the interior lights and keep the exterior lights on to make your car as visible as possible. Always stay inside the locked car and wait for assistance from the police. Do not open the door to a stranger.

You Know It's Time for a Tune-up When...

● It's difficult to start the car.
● It stalls frequently.
● You hear a knocking noise, generally when accelerating or climbing a hill.
● You lose power.

● You're getting poor gas mileage—you need to fill up more frequently.
● Your car is "dieseling"—the engine keeps sputtering for several seconds after the ignition is turned off.

● You experience exhaust odor—the smell of rotten eggs comes from the catalytic converter.
● The car runs rough—it shakes, for instance, when idling.

Tips for Tire Changers

A flat tire can occur at any time. While many people wait for roadside assistance, there may come a time when you have no choice but to change a tire yourself. These simple tips may help:

● Check your car's manual for proper placement of the jack. Never place the jack on a car part that can bend or break.

● Make sure the car is parked on level ground before you jack it up.

● Place bricks or rocks behind the wheels on the end of the car not being elevated to help prevent the car from rolling.

● Verify that your car is in "Park" with the emergency brake activated before you jack it up.

● Use a screwdriver to pry off the hubcap.

● If you have an aerosol tire-inflation kit, such as Fix-A-Flat, in your trunk, attach the nozzle to the valve stem of the flat tire and temporarily reinflate it. Proceed to the nearest service station for appropriate tire repair. Tell the mechanic you used an inflation product; the inside of the tire may need to be cleaned.

The Well-Equipped Trunk

The American Automobile Association suggests you always carry these items in your trunk:

✔ Jumper cables
✔ Flashlight and batteries
✔ Flares or reflective triangle
✔ Empty gas can
✔ Siphon hose
✔ Gallon of water or antifreeze
✔ Aerosol tire inflater
✔ Funnel
✔ Heavy-duty blanket or plastic sheeting
✔ Spare oil
✔ Electrician's tape
   (to fix disconnected hoses)
✔ Tow sign
✔ Spare tire and jack
✔ Work gloves
✔ Basic tools
   (screwdriver, wrench, pliers)
✔ First aid kit
✔ Windshield wiper fluid
✔ Nonperishable snacks
   (pretzels, nuts, or dried fruit)

Stash these winter storm supplies in your trunk when the weather starts to change:

✔ Sand or cat litter (to gain traction for snow- or ice-bound wheels)
✔ Collapsible snow shovel
✔ Lock de-icer
✔ Windshield scraper
✔ Tow chain or rope
✔ Extra cold-weather gear
✔ Chemical heat packs

Car Accident Record

NAME

ADDRESS

DRIVER'S LICENSE NO.

VEHICLE REGISTRATION NO.

CAR LICENSE PLATE NO.

INSURANCE COMPANY

POLICY NO.

PHONE NO.

WITNESS NAME

WITNESS PHONE NO.

WITNESS NAME

WITNESS PHONE NO.

WHAT HAPPENED

THE OTHER MOTORIST

NAME

ADDRESS

DRIVER'S LICENSE NO.

VEHICLE REGISTRATION NO.   CAR LICENSE PLATE NO.

INSURANCE COMPANY

POLICY NO.   PHONE NO.

WITNESS NAME   WITNESS PHONE NO.

WITNESS NAME   WITNESS PHONE NO.

WHAT HAPPENED

Snap Happy

How many times have you been in a situation where you thought, "If only I had a camera!" The new disposable varieties make it easy—and cost-effective—to keep one in every car. It'll come in handy if:

● You're ever in a minor traffic accident. You can take pictures of the scene and the damage, since it's usually difficult to remember all the facts clearly later on.

● You see a house or landscape you admire. Snap a picture so you can view it later to use as inspiration for your home or yard.

Sound Thinking

● Has this ever happened to you? Your car is making a funny noise as you drive, but when you take it to the mechanic, the car doesn't make the sound. Keep a tape recorder in the car with you so you can tape the sound the next time you hear it and play it back for your mechanic.

A picture is worth a thousand words, so keep a disposable camera in your car.

Clothes Care 101

If you're having too many "clothes encounters," read on.

I s "laundry" a dirty word in your house? For most of us, it's a never-ending struggle to stem the tide of unwashed, wrinkled, and need-to-be-mended clothes. (Do you feel as though they multiply overnight?) Well, don't get discouraged. The hints in this chapter will show you how to successfully tackle those wash-day woes, and our tips will help keep your clothes looking better and fresher longer.

Hamper Happenings

● Do your laundry hampers fill up faster than you can empty them? Try this: Give everyone in your family his or her own color-coded hamper or even a large clean plastic garbage can.

● Sprinkle some baking soda in the bottom of the clothes hamper to keep mildew off clothes and prevent smelly sweat socks from stinking up the hamper, possibly even the room.

Sorting It Out

● Keep at least four different color baskets or milk crates in the laundry room and label them as follows: "Whites," "Lights," "Darks," and "Delicates." Make family members sort their hamper clothes into these baskets.

● Sort clothes from the dryer into separate laundry baskets for each household member. This makes putting clothes away much easier, especially if everyone's responsible for his or her own laundry.

Prewash Winners

● Remember E-Z before loading laundry into the washer: E for "Empty pockets" and "Z" for "Zip all zippers."

● Fasten all hooks, such as those on bras,

before washing. Doing so protects other clothes, especially knits, from getting snagged and torn.

● Keep a supply of safety pins in the bedroom and laundry room and remind your family to pin their socks together before throwing them in the clothes hamper. This eliminates those "suddenly single" socks from materializing.

● Certain stains, usually protein based—baby formula, blood, egg, yogurt, milk, ice cream—will "set" when washed in warm water. Rinse or wash clothes with these stains in cool water, then treat the stain with a paste of meat tenderizer and water. Gently rub the paste on the stain, allow it to sit for a few minutes, then wash the item as usual.

● Keep a pretreat stain stick where most stains happen—in the kitchen—so you don't have to run to the laundry room every time you have a stain mishap.

Divide and conquer when it comes to sorting clothes from the dryer.

STAIN-SPECIFIC ADVICE

Here's a quick guide to removing common stains:

Blood A dab of 3 percent hydrogen peroxide solution removes blood stains from clothes.

Grease To get rid of a grease stain on a suede skirt or blouse, sprinkle some baking soda on the stain and then blot. Dry-clean as usual.

Gum If gum is stuck to an article of clothing, freeze the item, then carefully scrape the gum off with a dull knife.

Ink To get rid of ballpoint or felt-tip pen ink on a white shirt, use hair spray and a dab of liquid dish detergent. Rinse with cold water. Wash as usual.

Lipstick Lipstick stains on a collar? Rub out with a small washcloth that contains some alcohol. Or use baby wipes to remove lipstick stains from clothes. You can buy a small travel pack and tuck it in your purse or briefcase.

Oil Dirty hair and hands can leave behind an oily residue on shirt collars and cuffs. Use a bit of shampoo and water to remove the stain.

Paint If latex paint stains a fabric, immediately flush with warm water and wash as usual. For oil-base paint, gingerly apply paint thinner, then rinse with cool water.

Wine Pour plain (not fruit-flavored) carbonated water on a wine stain to dilute and bubble the stain out.

Yolk Soak a yolk-stained garment in cold water. Then rub with a paste of baking soda and water. Wash as usual.

Zinc oxide A pigment often found in cosmetics, sunscreen lotions, and acne creams, zinc oxide can leave a yellow stain on clothes. Pretreat the stain with a laundry product containing enzymes. Wash as usual.

Laundry List of Do's and Don'ts

DO'S	DON'TS
● Before using a chemical stain remover, pretest it on a nonvisible part of the garment. ● Remove as much of the stain as possible first by scraping or lifting but not rubbing. ● Always work the stain from the middle outward and handle the stained material gently. ● Never work on metal, plastic, or wooden surfaces; some chemicals stain these substances. Work on a glass surface.	● Never use heat or hot water on stained fabrics because these will "set" the stain. ● Don't use chemical cleaning agents in closed or unventilated rooms. ● Don't smoke. Don't use chemicals near open flames. Don't sniff chemicals. ● Never mix different agents unless directed to do so in instructions (you might create a caustic or poisonous mixture). ● Don't use caustic or solvent agents with bare hands—wear rubber gloves. ● Don't use undiluted vinegar on cottons or linens. ● Don't use alcohol on acrylics. ● Don't use enzymes on woolens, wool rugs, or silk.

Laundry Room Helpers

● For quick and easy access to your sheets of fabric softener, place the roll on an ordinary paper towel holder and hang the holder in your laundry room near the washer and dryer.

● If you run out of fabric-softener sheets or liquid fabric softener, put a drop or two of hair conditioner on a washcloth and toss it in with the clothes. They'll come out soft and smelling fresh.

● Hang a bulletin board near your washing machine and use it to hang clothing care labels, papers you find, and the like.

● Always check clothing labels for exceptions to the general rules for cleaning fabrics.

● Keep a paintbrush or toothbrush on the shelf with your laundry detergent. When you need to pretreat a stain, you can just dab some detergent on with the brush instead of wastefully pouring it right on the stain.

● To keep dark-colored garments lint-free, wash and hang them inside out until you're ready to wear.

Fiber Cleaning Fundamentals

Cashmere

● Dry-clean if woven. Hand-wash knits in cold water with baby shampoo or a detergent formulated for delicate fabrics. Lay flat to dry; use a cool iron if necessary. ● The long, soft hairs in high-quality cashmere actually become more luxurious with each hand washing. ● Never hang knits; fold them. ● Store in cedar.

Polyester

● Dry-clean or machine-wash. ● Dries fast, so use permanent-press cycle and remove as soon as possible to prevent wrinkles. ● If needed, iron on low setting.

Rayon or Tencel

● Hand-wash, machine-wash, or dry-clean, but check the label; manufacturers may add finishing touches that can affect the care. Machine-dry or hang-dry as indicated on the label. ● Stable; holds color and maintains fluid, draping character very well.

Silk

● Many "washable" and colorfast silks can be gently washed in lukewarm water. Keep the wash cycle short, and rinse quickly. Never use chlorine bleach, and don't let garments soak for long periods in water. ● If you dry-clean silk, be certain that the label recommends it; some silk dyes react to solvents. ● Hang-dry if woven; dry flat if knitted. ● Protect from sunlight and insects.

Wool

● Although wool is a stain-resistant fiber, you still need to treat a stain before it sinks in. Use a clean, damp sponge and blot—don't rub. ● Dry-clean as little as possible; once a season should be fine unless heavily worn. ● Wool retains its shape if folded carefully or hung on padded hangers. Never hang knits; fold them. ● Wool needs air and space to breathe. ● A steamy bathroom will remove most wrinkles.

Cotton

● If you're worried about shrinking, wash cotton in cold water; otherwise, it can withstand very hot temperatures. Avoid over-bleaching because it can wear down the fibers; every other wash is fine. Or try using white vinegar as a milder alternative to bleach. ● Takes longer to dry than most fabrics, so use a hot dryer setting and touch-test until dry. ● Responds well to a hot iron and doesn't easily scorch.

Wash Whiteners and Brighteners

● Here's a laundry technique you should try to get both your white and color loads clean and bright: Mix ¼ cup of your regular laundry detergent with ¼ cup ammonia in cold water. Then, to kill suds, add ¼ cup vinegar to the rinse water. Your whites will be bright, and colors won't fade.

● When washing new towels for the first time, add a cup of salt to the water. It will set the color so the towels won't fade as quickly.

Pressing Issues

● Your iron will glide smoothly over any type of fabric if you use it to "iron" a piece of waxed paper first, then move the hot iron over your wrinkled clothes. Don't worry, the waxed paper won't stain or stick to the garments.

● Put wet blouses and shirts on hangers and line-dry them by stringing chain instead of clothesline across the patio. The hangers' hooks fit into the chain links, and the clothes stay wrinkle-free and take up less space and drying time.

● It's the heat, not the weight, that removes wrinkles, so there is never any need to press an iron down hard, whether it's set on dry or steam.

● Start ironing from the middle of each garment section and work outward, pressing extra material toward the edges.

● Iron shirt collars last.

● Never iron in circular strokes,

Cleaning Techniques

Brushing Using a soft- or stiff-bristled brush (or toothbrush) to loosen and/or remove dried stains or to work in liquid or powder stain-removal agents.

Flushing Saturating the fabric with a cleaning agent or clean water.

Freezing Placing ice cubes on a stained material to harden the staining substance.

Presoaking or Soaking Placing the stained fabric in a stain-removal solution for a specific period of time. This is usually followed by a water rinse or laundering.

Scraping Removing excess stain with a stiff, dull knife or spatula.

Tamping Tapping or pounding the stain with a spoon handle or brush. (Be careful not to damage delicate fabrics.)

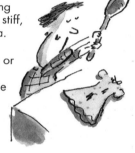

which will stretch out fabrics. Instead, iron lengthwise, carefully smoothing out the ridges. Iron bias-cut garments with the grain.

● If steam is called for, flatten wrinkles with a shot of steam.

● To save time, sort all your clothes according to the temperature settings they require. Then work from the coolest to the hottest, eliminating the need to wait for the iron to cool down between temperature settings.

● Always iron silks on the wrong side. This will help prevent an unattractive sheen, especially along seams or pocket edges.

Best Bets for Buttons, Zippers, and Bows

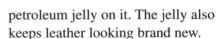

● Apply a thin coat of clear nail polish or nail hardener to mother-of-pearl–finished buttons in order to restore luster and make them stronger and more durable.

● A drop or two of clear nail polish on button threads will make them stronger and keep buttons in place longer.

Give new life to old ribbon with spray starch and a curling iron.

● Here's a trick for fixing metal zippers that stick: Rub candle wax along the teeth, then press with an iron.

● To keep ribbons on a party dress from fraying, brush clear nail polish on the ends and sides. You'll find that the ribbons will hold up in the wash.

● Restore tired ribbons to like-new condition: First spray with a bit of spray starch, then "press" with a curling iron.

Head-to-Toe Helpers

● To clean those grungy-looking baseball caps that kids (and many grown-ups) now wear, put them in the top rack of your dishwasher and run through a regular wash.

● You can air-dry those caps on a 3-pound coffee can. The baseball cap will dry quickly and retain its shape beautifully.

● To remove scuff marks from shoes, use a wool mitten with a bit of petroleum jelly on it. The jelly also keeps leather looking brand new.

● You can also use a dab of nonabrasive toothpaste to remove stubborn scuff marks from leather and vinyl shoes.

● The secret to removing scuff marks from dress shoes: Gently rub the mark with a cotton ball soaked in nail polish remover.

● Petroleum jelly easily removes tar and sap from the soles of your shoes.

Scents and Sensibility

● If you love to wear perfume but hesitate to spray it on for fear of spotting your clothes, try this: Just before pressing your blouses, trousers, and skirts, spritz your ironing board with perfume. The steam from the iron draws just a whisper of the scent, which will cling to the fabric all day.

Static Magic

● After you've massaged a dollop or two of hand lotion into your hands, gently rub them over the panty hose you're wearing to control static cling.

Odor Beater

● To remove cigarette odor from a blouse, skirt, or slacks, place a dryer fabric-softener sheet on the hanger with the garment and cover it with a plastic bag. The cigarette odor will be gone by morning.

Lint Removers

● If you can't find a lint brush, use a piece of fine-grain sandpaper to remove lint from your clothes.

● A damp clean sponge makes a fine lint remover, especially when you're ironing. The lint comes off easily, and the sponge dampens the fabric, which makes wrinkles come out more easily too.

Storing Savvy

● Plastic dry-cleaning bags are great for enclosing clothes when you travel, but don't use them on everyday closet items. Left on over time, the plastic contributes to mildew and discoloration.

● Use padded hangers for jackets and shirts; always close a few buttons. Stuff tissue paper into the arms and between folds to prevent creasing.

● Make sure cedar, mothballs, or moth crystals have a pungent aroma. That's what repels insects.

● On the other hand, moths are attracted to your scent! Be sure clothes are clean and free of body odor before storing them.

Folding Facts

Once your clothes are cleaned and pressed, the last thing you want to do is wrinkle them as you're putting them away. This four-step process works with blouses, T-shirts, or sweaters.

1. Lay flat, front down, and crisscross the sleeves over the back.

2. Fold in one side, smoothing as you go. To avoid deep creases, cushion the fold with tissue paper—or with lingerie if packing in a suitcase.

3. Repeat with the other side.

4. Fold up the bottom; gently turn over. (When storing several tops, note that heavy stacking may press in creases.)

Stain-Removal Chart

Take each step only as needed to remove the stain. Test for colorfastness on an inconspicuous area of the garment first. After treating the garment, launder or dry-clean as usual.

WHAT TO HAVE ON HAND

✔ **Alcohol** Denatured or rubbing. Do not use on acrylic, acetate, or triacetate.

✔ **Ammonia** Household. Do not use on wool or silk.

✔ **Amyl acetate** (available at drugstores) or nonoily nail polish remover.

✔ **Bleach** Chlorine if care label of material allows; if not, all-fabric.

✔ **Detergent** Liquid dishwashing.

✔ **Dry-cleaning solvent** (available at drugstores and grocery stores)

✔ **Dry spotter** 1 part coconut oil (available at drugstores) or mineral oil and 8 parts dry-cleaning solvent. Store in glass container with tight-fitting lid.

✔ **Enzyme product** Enzyme presoak or laundry detergent.

✔ **Vinegar** White.

✔ **Wet spotter** 1 part glycerin (available at drugstores), 1 part liquid dishwashing detergent, and 8 parts water. Shake well; store in plastic squeeze bottle.

STAIN	STAIN REMOVER
Alcoholic beverages, wine, cough syrup, coffee, fruit, soda, tea, vegetables	**Washables:** **1.** Sponge with cool water. **2.** Soak in solution of 1 quart warm water, ½ teaspoon detergent, and 1 tablespoon vinegar; rinse with water. (Red wine: Flush with alcohol.) **Nonwashables:** **1.** Flush with cool water. **2.** Apply wet spotter with a few drops of vinegar; blot with clean cloth or paper towel. (Red wine: Rinse with lukewarm water. Blot with alcohol.)
Car wax, crayon, grease, lard, makeup, tar, ink (other than ballpoint), margarine, paint	**Washables and Nonwashables:** **1.** Sponge with dry-cleaning solvent. **2.** Cover with absorbent material moistened with dry spotter; blot occasionally. **3.** Flush with dry-cleaning solvent; let dry. Sponge with water. **4.** Blot with wet spotter with a few drops of ammonia; flush with water.

STAIN	STAIN REMOVER
Baby food, cheese sauces, chocolate, egg, gravy, ice cream, ketchup, milk, steak or chili sauces, vegetable soups	**Washables:** **1.** Sponge with cold water. **2.** Cover with pad (folded cloth or paper towels) moistened with dry spotter; blot occasionally. **3.** Flush with dry-cleaning solvent; let dry. **4.** Sponge with water; apply a few drops of detergent and a few drops of ammonia. Flush with water. **5.** Soak in solution of 1 quart warm water and 1 tablespoon enzyme product. Rinse with water. **Nonwashables:** **1.** Try steps 1–4 above. **2.** Cover with pad dampened with mix of ½ teaspoon enzyme product and ½ cup warm water for 30 minutes. Flush with water.
Blood, meat soups, mucus, vomit	**Washables:** **1.** Soak in cold water. **2.** Soak in solution of 1 quart warm water, ½ teaspoon detergent, and 1 tablespoon ammonia; blot. **3.** Soak in 1 quart water with 1 tablespoon enzyme product. **Nonwashables:** **1.** Sponge with cold water. **2.** Cover with pad moistened with wet spotter and a few drops of ammonia. **3.** Moisten with ½ teaspoon enzyme product in ½ cup warm water.
Deodorant, perspiration, red ink or watercolor paints, urine, red dyes	**Washables:** **1.** Soak in cold water. **2.** Soak in solution of 1 quart warm water, ½ teaspoon detergent, and 1 tablespoon ammonia for 30 minutes; rinse with water; let dry. **3.** Cover with alcohol-dampened pad; blot. **Nonwashables:** **1.** Sponge with cold water. **2.** Cover with pad moistened with wet spotter and a few drops of ammonia; blot; flush with water. **3.** Apply wet spotter with a few drops of vinegar; blot; flush with water. **4.** Apply alcohol; flush with water.

STAIN	STAIN REMOVER
Oils (vegetable and fish), butter, chewing gum	**Washables and Nonwashables:** Oil stain: Sprinkle with baby powder to absorb; brush off before treating. Gum: Rub with ice cube or place in freezer to harden; scrape off excess with spoon before treating. **1.** Place cloth under stain; cover with pad dampened with dry-cleaning fluid; remove. **2.** Cover with clean pad moistened with dry spotter; remove. **3.** Flush with dry-cleaning solvent; let dry.
Bluing, fabric and hair dyes, food coloring, vegetable colors, watercolor paints	**Washables:** **1.** Soak in solution of 1 quart warm water, ½ teaspoon detergent, and 1 tablespoon vinegar; rinse; let dry. **2.** Cover with pad moistened with alcohol; blot; flush with alcohol; let dry. **3.** Soak in solution of 1 quart warm water, ½ teaspoon detergent, and 1 tablespoon ammonia; rinse with water. **Nonwashables:** **1.** Sponge with cool water. **2.** Apply wet spotter with a few drops of vinegar; blot; flush with water; let dry. **3.** Cover with pad moistened with alcohol; blot; flush with alcohol; sponge with water. **4.** Apply wet spotter with a few drops of ammonia; flush with water.
Pen ink (ballpoint)	**Washables and Nonwashables:** **1.** Apply lukewarm glycerin; blot; flush with water. **2.** Apply wet spotter; blot. **3.** Add several drops of ammonia; blot; flush with water.
Unknown stains	**Washables and Nonwashables:** **1.** Sponge with dry-cleaning solvent. **2.** Apply dry spotter. **3.** Flush with dry-cleaning solvent. Repeat steps 1–3 as needed. **4.** Apply amyl acetate. **5.** Flush with dry-cleaning solvent; let dry. **6.** Sponge with water; add wet spotter with a few drops of vinegar; let dry.

International Care Symbols

This chart will help you decipher the proper care and cleaning your clothes need to keep them looking their best.

WASHING

	Normal		Do Not Wash
	Permanent Press	•••	50°C 120°F
	Delicate/ Gentle	••	40°C 105°F
	Hand-wash	•	30°C 85°F

DRYCLEANING

(A)	Any Solvent		Short Cycle
(P)	Any Solvent Except Trichloroethylene		Reduce Moisture
(F)	Fluorocarbon or Petroleum Solvent Only		Low Heat
	Do Not Dry-clean		No Steam Finishing

BLEACHING

△	Any Bleach When Needed
⚠	Only Nonchlorine Bleach When Needed
	Do Not Bleach

IRONING

	200°C/390°F high
	150°C/300°F medium
	110°C/230°F low
	No Steam
	Do Not Iron

DRYING

	Normal	(•••)	High		Line-dry/ Hang	●	No Heat/Air
	Permanent Press	(••)	Medium	III	Drip-dry		Do Not Wring
	Delicate/ Gentle	(•)	Low	—	Dry Flat		Do Not Tumble-dry

YOUR SELF

"Enjoy yourself — it's later than you think."

Chinese Proverb

Tension Tamers

While we can't eliminate every source of stress from your life, we can give you tried-and-true ways to keep energy-sapping anxiety from getting the best of you. Sometimes it takes only a soothing cup of tea or a 10-minute soak in the tub to restore your sense of calm and boost your energy level. Remember, being good to yourself is good for everyone around you too.

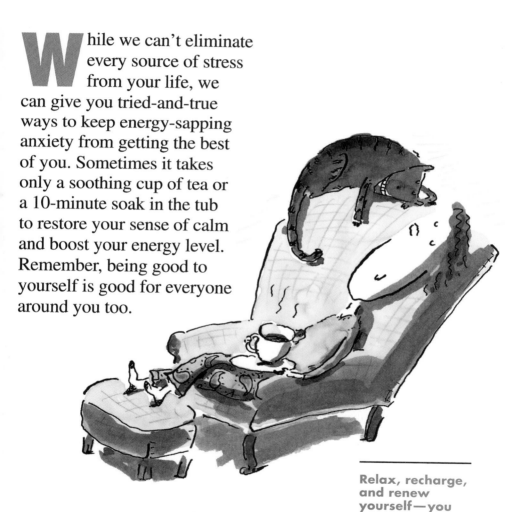

Relax, recharge, and renew yourself—you are your most valuable resource.

Soothing Soaks

● Set the scene for a soothing soak. Dim the lights, illuminate the bathroom with candles, then put on some soothing music. Try romantic or classical music to ease you into a relaxed state.

● Wash your cares and woes away by slipping into a warm (not hot!) tub of frothy bubbles and feel the tension dissolve. To relax your muscles, the water temperature should be lower than your body temperature—try 78 degrees.

● Cradle your head on a cushy bath pillow or a soft folded towel as you enjoy this soothing eye treatment: Place chilled, steeped chamomile tea bags on your lids (the herb helps reduce puffiness). In 5 to 10 minutes, remove the tea bags and give your body a fragrant cleansing. Wet a loofah with bath gel and gently buff your skin.

● For an instant pick-me-up either at home or on the job, lean over a sink and splash your face with cool water. You can even keep a small spray bottle of water and witch hazel in your handbag, backpack, or car to spray your face lightly. The refreshing clean scent will revive you.

● A shower can be invigorating and energizing when you alternate warm and cool water. To avoid shocking your body, shift gradually between the warm and cool water temperatures two or three times during the shower. For a final zing, end your shower with a cold-water rinse.

● To moisturize and cleanse: Mix 3 cups uncooked oatmeal and 2 cups wheat bran, then stir in ¼ cup liquid body soap or gel. Spoon the mixture

Soak your worries away. No one ever comes out of a bath more stressed than she went in.

into the foot portion of old (clean) panty hose or a knee-high sock or into a square of fine-mesh cheesecloth. Tie the bag with a string, drop it into a tub full of warm water (98 to 100 degrees), and let it—and you—soak for a bit. Rub the bag all over your body to gently cleanse and rejuvenate your skin.

● To release emotional stress: Fill the tub one-quarter full with hot water (101 degrees) and 1 cup noniodized salt or Epsom salts. Step into the tub and lie down in the water, continuing to let the water run until it's to your chin level. Close your eyes for 5 to 10 minutes. Follow the soaking bath with a cool shower.

● If your muscles are tied up in knots, add some lavender-scented sachets to your bath or try a lavender-oil massage.

● To soothe sore, aching muscles, toss in a handful of Epsom salts.

● Sprinkle rose petals in your bath. Ancient wisdom holds that the scent of roses brings on a happier frame of mind. No petals? A few drops of rose oil will do.

● Add a cup of plain vinegar to your bathwater to eliminate itching dry skin.

● Treat yourself to a milk bath: Make 3 quarts hot milk from dry-milk powder and add 1 cup honey and 1 cup chamomile tea. Mix these and add to the bath. Mmmm, good. (For other herbal stress relievers, see *Calming Scents,* page 173.)

Meditation Time

● Take a 5-minute respite from the daily grind by meditating. Here's how: Put on some soothing music or a tape of nature sounds (ocean waves, gentle rain). Sit in a comfortable chair, shut your eyes, and visualize a peaceful place where you'd love to be, or think about a favorite inspirational verse. Inhale slowly and deeply for two counts; then exhale more slowly, for four counts. If your mind drifts, follow your thoughts and gently redirect them to your peaceful place or verse.

● Another option: With eyes closed, sit quietly and hold a small stone or a seashell in one palm. Run your fingers slowly over the object, feeling its texture and shape. As you do this, picture the object in your mind's eye. Empty your mind of any other thoughts until you are concentrating only on what's in your hand.

Mentally take yourself to another place.

Work Out Your Stress

● Put on some snappy music and dance your cares away. Let the sound of the music carry you to another place. Dancing will lift your spirits and energize you at the same time.

● It's been clinically proven that regular exercise improves the spirit as well as the mind. Join a gym and incorporate an exercise program into your weekly routines so that feeling good becomes a habit.

● Whenever you can, walk rather than ride. Letting your mind wander as you walk is meditative. Look around you and take note, as if you were a tourist and this were the first time you had ever seen the area. It's amazing how refreshing it is to look anew at what is familiar and to discover what you may never have noticed before. Meanwhile, your mind is far away from what has caused you stress.

● While moderate exercise reduces stress, overdoing it can create other kinds of stress. If you feel exhausted rather than exhilarated after a workout, you're pushing yourself too hard. Ease up to enjoy the benefits.

Words Work Too!

● Create a list of everything positive about yourself—physical traits, special talents, character assets. Don't be shy. Seeing your positive attributes listed on a page boosts self-esteem and pumps up your self-confidence. Tuck the list in your wallet or pocket, and whenever you need encouragement, reread it.

● To help recharge your batteries, treat yourself to a cup of fragrant herb tea and curl up with a best-seller or

Remind yourself with a list of how special you really are.

favorite magazine. Even if it's for only 20 minutes, allow yourself to escape to another world.

● Copy a favorite saying or poem in your best penmanship or fanciest printing and think about each word as you write. Post it in a spot where you're most likely to feel overwhelmed—by the kitchen phone or over your desk at work, for example. Take 5 minutes out of each day to reread the words and reflect on their meaning and importance to you.

● Make a wish list of things you want to do or places you want to go. Clip out magazine articles and pictures of your plans and destinations and store them in a folder or book. Concentrating on your private desire helps you feel fulfilled and provides you with more energy for coping with everyone else's needs.

Color Your World

● To reduce stress, surround yourself with calming colors—soft blues, gentle greens, pale pinks, for example. Or if you're feeling down, give yourself an energy lift by wearing warm colors—vibrant orange, bright yellow, or fire-engine red—for maximum impact. You don't necessarily have to swathe yourself in these colors; sometimes a pretty accent piece—a scarf, bracelet, or gloves—is enough to give you the lift you need.

● Feeling blue? Try a rich, red lipstick to awaken your whole face. Treat yourself to a new shade and watch how positive the response is when you put your best face forward.

Back to Nature

● Working with plants is a time-tested stress buster, so prune a houseplant or hoe your garden and reap the rewards when the plants begin to show their appreciation.

● Fill a vase with pretty blooms you've either grown yourself or purchased from a farmer's market or florist. Take time to arrange the blossoms in a vase, and place the vase in a very visible spot where you'll see it often.

The Healing Power of Touch

Massage unknots muscles, stimulates circulation, and releases endorphins, the brain's feel-good chemicals. Don't have a massage therapist on call? Do it yourself.

● Work your fingertips in circular motions along your forehead and over your scalp. Move down along the nape of your neck and shoulders.

● Tired eyes? With one thumb and forefinger at the top of the bridge of your nose, make soothing circles, moving out along your brow lines.

● If your back is tight, work on the webbed section of your hand between your thumb and index finger. Grasp with the thumb and a finger of the opposite hand and press. Release, move your thumb higher on the web, and press again. Continue until you are at the top of the web. Now repeat the process in the opposite direction.

7-MINUTE TENSION TAMER

● This acupressure massage takes just 7 minutes but will ease tension for hours. Do each step for 1 minute.

1. Place your index fingers on your hairline, 1 inch apart, directly above your eyes. Move your fingers in inward circles.

2. Bring your fingers down to just above the brows, pressing them into the bone and rubbing in inward circles.

3. Place your thumbs inside the brow bone, resting against the eye sockets. Rotate your thumbs toward your nose—avoid pressing on your eyes.

4. Place your index fingers at the outer ends of your brows; move them around in outward circles.

5. Place your index fingers on the eye-socket bone under your pupil; make outward circles.

6. Smile and place your index fingers on the apples of your cheeks; make outward circles.

7. Place your fingers on the cleft between your nose and lips; make inward circles.

Treat Your Feet

● The ancient healing art of reflexology uses massage on certain areas of the feet to promote well-being in corresponding parts of the body. One technique to try: Press your thumbs on the soles of your feet, right at the center. Circle your thumbs around and around. You'll love how you feel all over. To heighten alertness, tackle your big toes.

● Give yourself a "secret" foot massage. Keep a firm rubber ball under your desk at work (or beneath your favorite easy chair at home), and rub your foot over it, from heel to toe.

TERRIFIC TOE TINGLER

● Here's a wonderful foot massage, from the Norwich Inn & Spa in Norwich, Connecticut, that's guaranteed to please. Do each step on each foot before proceeding to the next step. Use a moisturizer or a base oil, such as olive, sweet almond, or sesame, to make the rubbing a bit smoother. If you like, add a bit of your favorite scent to the base oil.

1. Rub each foot quickly with both hands to warm it and accustom it to your touch.

2. Take one foot in both hands and stroke the arch with both thumbs pointing toward the ball of the foot. Then repeat this procedure on the other foot.

3. Still using your thumbs, work your way up toward the ball of the foot.

4. Press your thumbs along both the inside and outside edges of the foot. With both hands, quickly flex each foot up at the ankle and then stretch it away from the ankle.

5. Run your knuckles up and down the bottom of your foot.

6. With both hands, gently flex and stretch each foot at the ankle.

Face Facts

● Indulge in a facial and you'll feel better all over. This homemade citrus mask refreshes and tones: Blend 2 tablespoons each of lemon and orange juice; fold in an egg white and beat until foamy. Apply to your face; leave on 20 minutes, then rinse with warm water.

● Or try this mix: ¼ to ½ cup yogurt (plain, apple, banana, or strawberry) with 3 tablespoons uncooked oatmeal. Blend into a paste, adding more oatmeal if needed. Apply to your face, lie down, and leave on 5 to 10 minutes. Remove by gently rubbing with a washcloth and warm water.

● Here's one of the easiest tricks of all: Cool cucumber slices placed on tired eyes soothe and reduce swelling of the lids and below the eyes. And it's fascinating how much more relaxed you'll feel afterward.

● Smile! It sounds obvious, but smiling—even when you don't feel like it—helps elevate your mood and tends to ease the people around you at the same time.

Cucumber slices cool tired eyes.

Calming Scents

How often has just one whiff of a favorite fragrance changed your mood? Fragrance acts on receptors in your nose to signal the release of calming chemicals in the brain. You can use herbs, essential oils (mixed first with water or vegetable oil), or skin-care products that include the potent essences listed below. Refer to this chart to select an appealing stress-relieving scent.

ESSENCE	FRAGRANCE	EFFECTS	USES
Chamomile	Fresh, herbaceous, with sweet undertones	Calms, reduces inflammation.	Sprinkle a few drops in steaming water; inhale.
Ginger	Fiery, spicy	Energizes, warms.	Mix with oil to massage on tired muscles; blend with orange for warming winter baths.
Lavender	Clean, balsamic, herbaceous, with floral, woodsy undertones	Eases headaches and anxiety.	Rub on temples or toss into bathwater; keep a sachet by your bedside.
Lemongrass	Sweet, powerful, "lemony" aroma	Calms, cleanses.	Refreshing, stimulating tonic on the body. Added to shampoos, enhances shine on hair.
Peppermint	Invigorating, distinctly minty, with cooling menthol notes	Stimulates; soothes limbs.	Stroke on as lotion or add to your bath.
Rose geranium	Floral rose with minty undertones	Boosts alertness, lifts mood.	Mingle with massage oil; mix dried leaves with potpourri.
Sandalwood	Sweet, rich, warm, woodsy tones	Calms, cleanses.	Dab on as perfume or use chips in bath herb blends.

● Likewise, laughter can lift the spirits and ease physical tension. Take time out to read a humorous book, watch a TV or film comedy, listen to a funny audiotape—whatever gets you chuckling.

Body Rubs

● A body mask leaves your skin oh-so-silky smooth. Take a handful of crushed almonds, add 5 tablespoons uncooked oatmeal, 2 teaspoons brown sugar, 2 tablespoons honey, and ¼ cup hot water, and mix into a paste. Slather this mixture onto your shoulders, arms, back—everywhere you can reach. Leave on the mask for 10 minutes, then massage it in and rinse off with warm water. Follow up with an application of body lotion.

Pet Your Pet

● It's a fact that stroking your cat or playing with your dog reduces blood pressure, relieves stress, and improves your mood.

Just Say No

● It may sound simplistic, but for those of us who overload ourselves with responsibility, saying no is the easiest way to preserve and conserve energy for the things that really matter to us. Need a nice way to turn down that next committee? Say, "Thank you for asking me. I would *love* to help, but I'm truly overloaded at the moment. When I'm less booked, I'll get in touch with you."

Sleep Matters

● Lack of sleep leaves you tired, cranky, and you guessed it, more prone to stress. Be good to yourself—

Animal lovers, rejoice! Pets can keep you healthy.

rejuvenate your body with a minimum of 7 to 8 hours of shut-eye every night.
● You'll fall asleep more easily if you unwind for at least an hour before bedtime. Don't tackle stress-inducing tasks like balancing your checkbook or making a to-do list just before bed. Vigorous exercise will overexcite you and your body and make it harder to get to sleep. Also, steer clear of alcohol as a way of downshifting. Alcohol actually interferes with sleep patterns; while it might make you drowsy initially, it is actually a stimulant that will accelerate your heartbeat and possibly awaken you in the middle of the night.
● Unlike alcohol, certain herbal teas (such as chamomile) will help you sleep, as will a cup of warm milk consumed before bedtime.
● Never underestimate the power of a nap. Sometimes just 20 minutes of shut-eye during the day can give you the lift you need to carry on.
● Feel a yawn coming on? Don't suppress it. Yawning helps bring needed oxygen into your bloodstream. In fact, you can enhance the benefits of a yawn by getting up to stretch at the same time.

Early Morning Stretch

● Before you get out of bed in the morning, elongate your body by stretching your arms over your head and extending your legs by pointing your toes. Hold this stretch for 10 seconds. Relax your feet; bring your arms to your sides.

● Lift one leg toward the ceiling, pulling it toward your chest with your hands. Hold for 10 seconds. Repeat with the other leg.

● Sit up slowly, vertebra by vertebra, reaching your arms toward your feet. If you can, grab your toes and hold for 10 seconds. Relax. Take a deep breath. Exhale. Repeat. Now you're ready to start your day.

Breathing Easy

● It's a fact: Tense, nervous people breathe in short shallow breaths, while calm, relaxed people take in their air slowly and deeply. Limiting your air intake deprives you of the amount of oxygen you need in the bloodstream. This, in turn, fails to reduce the level of carbon dioxide, causing blood vessels to constrict. As a result, less oxygen gets to your brain, which results in feelings of nervousness and tension. To increase the level of oxygen in your system and reduce your feelings of stress, practice this deep-breathing technique:

1. Pay attention to your posture. Sit or lie comfortably with your back straight. The less hunched you are when you do your breathing exercises, the more air you can take into your lungs. Relax

your shoulders, arms, and legs.

2. Inhale deeply through your nostrils for a count of 4, so that the air fills the bottom of your lungs. Hint: If your shoulders move when you do this, you are not breathing in correctly. Only your abdomen should expand. Hold your breath for the count of 7.

3. Exhale slowly through your mouth for a count of 8. *Note: A calm person takes 6 to 8 breaths per minute. That should be your goal.*

4. Repeat the breathing exercise for a total of 4 cycles. Breathe normally and see how your body feels.

Watchful Ideas

● Don't watch the clock, especially if you're sitting in traffic or standing in line. Watching the minutes tick by only adds to your tension level.

● Leave your wristwatch at home one day and see what happens if you just follow your natural impulses: Eat when you're hungry, rest when you're tired. Learn your body's natural rhythms and work with them. You will go through the day with a lot less stress.

Muscle-by-Muscle Relaxation

Try this technique if your muscles get tense from too much stress:

● Lie down on a comfortable surface, such as a mat or rug.

● Inhale and squeeze your right foot and leg tightly, raising them slightly from the floor. Exhale and relax your foot and leg.

● Repeat with your left leg. Do the same tightening and releasing exercise with your abdomen, buttocks, arms, and finally neck and jaw. Remember to inhale when your are tensing your muscles, exhale when you relax them.

Affirming Thoughts

● Repeating a word or phrase rhythmically over and over can often induce the state of relaxation. Choose a word or phrase that means something to you: "I am confident" or "calm"; "I am relaxed" or "happy"; or choose a phrase that expresses your spiritual beliefs. Begin by breathing deeply. Then repeat the word or phrase out loud if you're at home or alone in the car, or silently in your head. Say the word or phrase repeatedly, and focus on it if your mind begins to wander. It is believed that if you repeat these positive phrases to yourself several times a day, they will infiltrate your subconscious and produce a positive outcome.

● Spend some time each day writing in a journal. This is a wonderful way to vent your feelings, express your desires, focus your thoughts, or allow them to flow stream-of-consciousness style. There's no right or wrong way to keep a journal, but the more consistent you can be about keeping it, the more effective it becomes as a tool for clarifying your thoughts.

Social Swirl

● Get together with friends at least once a week and let your hair down. Enjoy a movie, lunch, or Sunday brunch with your pals. Make a regular date for weekly walks together.

Mood Foods

What you eat can affect how you function. Need energy for an afternoon meeting? Eat a protein-packed lunch. Carbohydrates, on the other hand, can have a calming, tension-easing effect. Here are some healthy options.

PROTEIN PUNCHES	HIGH-CARBO SOOTHERS
✔ Water-packed tuna straight from the can or mixed with tomato	✔ Animal crackers
✔ Lean deli ham or turkey wrapped around a celery stick (for crunch) to dip into mustard	✔ Air-popped popcorn
✔ Low-fat or nonfat yogurt	✔ Fresh bagel
✔ Hard-boiled egg	✔ Low-fat or nonfat sorbet or sherbet
✔ Mozzarella string cheese	✔ English muffin
✔ Turkey burger with lots of lettuce and tomato	✔ Breadsticks
✔ Low-fat chocolate milk	✔ Pretzels
✔ Peanut-butter cheese-cracker sandwiches (but only one or two occasionally—they're high in fat)	✔ Pasta with marinara sauce
✔ Veggie pizza	✔ Pancakes with fruit and maple syrup
	✔ Small portion of take-out stir-fried rice with vegetables
	✔ Pita pocket stuffed with veggies
	✔ Plain baked potato

Unwind Time

- Find some quiet time every day, even if it's only half an hour.
- Laughter truly is a stress reliever. Go see a stand-up comic, read a funny book, or watch a silly movie.
- Escape into a romantic novel or mystery, nothing reality based.
- Sing! That's right, even if you can't carry a tune, singing at the top of your lungs not only improves your mood but also forces you to breathe deeply, a proven tension tamer (see *Breathing Easy,* page 175).

Does Your Space Say "Calm"?

Haphazardly arranged or cluttered spaces are not relaxing. If you take some care to arrange your furnishings, you can create a pleasingly harmonious atmosphere that feels balanced—which will help you to feel calm or energized, as you wish. Here are some tips to help you do this; as you apply them, think of how the room "flows," or more simply, whether it feels right to you.

- The entranceway to your home or office should be open and inviting. Trim back plants to prevent them from obstructing the entrance.
- When natural light is unavailable in a hallway or vestibule, make sure the space is well illuminated.
- Arrange the furniture in your living room and family room so that, when seated, everyone faces one another. This encourages open conversation.
- Always position a bed, desk, or stove so that it faces the door.

- Keep kitchen counters and other work surfaces free of clutter to create a space that is both serene and efficient.
- Mirrors increase the sense of space and make dark areas seem lighter.
- Plants and flowers bring life into your home or office. Choose plants that have round leaves.

Food for Thought

- Try as we might, we don't always eat right, and stress can actually leach vital nutrients from our bodies, so consider taking vitamin supplements, such as a multivitamin. If you're a vegetarian, you probably need to take an iron supplement every day too.
- A good breakfast—one that sustains you throughout the morning—is vital

Get your day off to a good start with a balanced breakfast.

to maintaining your energy level. Complex carbohydrates—bread, potatoes, cereal—release their fuel slowly, especially when combined with some protein, such as low-fat cottage cheese. Try a bowl of hot oatmeal with a sprinkling of pecans and raisins to start your day.

● Although coffee and caffeine products can temporarily jolt you out of a slump, more than a cup or two can be counterproductive, resulting in increased heartbeat and elevated blood pressure. In addition, too much caffeine may make you feel edgy and less equipped to handle even small crises. Instead, drink caffeine-free herbal teas or refreshing water flavored with fruit or mint leaves.

● When the pressure is on, do you reach for those no-no snacks? Foods high in fat, such as ice cream, pastries, or french fries, actually slow you down, making you feel sluggish. Instead, nosh on foods with protein, which quells serotonin, the brain chemical that can induce sleepiness.

● For a quick pick-me-up between meals, pop a mint into your mouth. Whether it's in the form of a hard candy, breath spray, or mouthwash, mint refreshes and revives you.

● Orange juice may seem like a great refresher, but its high concentration of carbohydrates makes it just the opposite. The carbohydrate is so quickly absorbed that a slump follows the rush. Instead, consume whole oranges. They are rich in fiber, which the body absorbs more gradually.

● When you need to unwind, carbohydrates are the foods to reach for. They enable tryptophan, a calming amino acid, to enter the brain easily. Once there, tryptophan raises levels of serotonin, which not only relaxes you but also seems to help your mind focus.

Healthy Herbs

Herbal healers come in several forms: bulk-dried plant material, teas, tablets, and tinctures (alcohol or glycerin extracts). Except for beverage herbs (chamomile, ginger), most herbalists recommend tinctures, which are available at health food stores. The herbs below are generally considered safe if you follow package directions.

Chamomile tea can be applied as a compress to soothe skin irritations and infections. Taken internally, it calms abdominal distress.

Echinacea stimulates the immune system to help fight colds, flu, and other infections.

Garlic helps lower cholesterol and prevents the blood clots that trigger heart attacks.

Gingko biloba improves blood flow through the brain.

Ginseng, a root, helps the body resist damage from physical or emotional stress and old age.

Goldenseal stimulates the immune system and has antibacterial and antifungal actions. It also is used to treat respiratory infections.

St. John's wort acts as a mild antidepressant.

Valerian, a root, is available as an herbal sleeping pill.

CHAPTER 14

Diet and Fitness Made Easy

If just trying to figure out how and when you can work out causes you to break into a sweat, or if the mere suggestion of a "healthy" food has your family heading for the hills, these hints and tips are for you! We'll give you ways to "sneak" those fruits and vegetables into foods so that even your family won't suspect they're good for them.

Worked up over the thought of working out? A healthy lifestyle is within your reach.

Better Breakfasts

● Switch from 2 percent to skim milk. If you drink a cup every day, the fat difference is almost 32 grams a week. If you feel that skim milk turns your coffee gray, try lactose-free milk. It has the same fat-free content, but it seems richer.

● Hate the look and taste of skim milk in your coffee? Put your normal amount of skim milk in a coffee mug and heat it in the microwave for 10 to 20 seconds, just until it gets "frothy." Then add the coffee to the milk. It tastes creamier and has more eye appeal.

● Want to cut out a quick 60 calories first thing in the morning? Instead of gulping down a glass of orange juice, eat an orange or half a grapefruit. Not only do you get the benefit of that much-needed vitamin C, but you also fill up on good-for-you fiber.

Whole fruit is a healthier option than juice.

● Love eggs in the morning but need to watch your cholesterol? Make an omelet with one egg and one egg white. By eliminating the second egg yolk, you'll save more than 250 mg of cholesterol and 65 calories. Removing both egg yolks, of course, will save even more!

● Fill that omelet with steamed vegetables and herbs instead of cheese, and you'll shave off another 210 calories and about 16 grams of fat per 2 ounces of cheese.

● Tired of just plain old grapefruit for breakfast? Cut a grapefruit in half, sprinkle the top with cinnamon and a half teaspoon brown sugar, then broil on low for 5 minutes. Tastes like a dessert!

● If your kids are a little too liberal with the sugar on their morning breakfast cereal, make it easier for them to "see" what they're doing — mix a few drops of food coloring into the sugar bowl. The brightly colored sweetener is easier to spot in the milk-covered cereal, and they'll be less likely to overdo it.

● Here is another way to beat the sweet habit: Put the colored sugar in a salt shaker—just a few shakes is all it takes.

● Premix unsweetened cereal with a small amount of your kids' favorite sweetened cereal. Your kids get their sugar fix, but you get to control how much of the sweet stuff they eat.

● Allow toast to cool before you butter it. That way, less butter will be absorbed.

French Toast and Pancakes

● Cook French toast or pancakes in a nonstick skillet or on a griddle coated with nonstick cooking spray.

● Substitute half of the milk in each batter with plain nonfat yogurt.

● Puree fresh fruit in a blender and use as a syrup substitute.

● No fresh fruit in the house? Keep a few jars of pureed baby food fruit and use that as a spread.

● Chunky unsweetened applesauce also makes a nice topper for pancakes and waffles. Heat it in the microwave first.

Say yes to this soda made with one part seltzer and two parts juice.

Having Your Cake . . . and Fewer Calories Too

● For many cake and cookie recipes, you can replace some of the fat with applesauce or prune puree. The taste will be virtually unchanged, but you'll cut out significant calories and fat.

● You can usually eliminate part or even all of the oil from the ingredients to be added to a store-bought cake mix. You may need to add more water or another egg to make up the liquid shortfall, but the taste and texture will usually be unaffected.

Soda Substitute

● If your kids love soft drinks but you don't want them consuming too many, try this trick: Mix one part seltzer and two parts fruit juice to create a fizzy beverage your kids will love.

● Clear water is far superior to soft drinks. Since it's important to drink water throughout the day—eight 8-ounce glasses is recommended—fill up a 2-quart pitcher or several water bottles first thing in the morning and drink from them all day long. After a while, consuming eight glasses a day will become second nature.

● Downing a big glass of water before each meal or a party will take the edge off your appetite. You'll feel more full—and more in control of your hunger.

● To give ordinary water some extra pizzazz, add some cut-up fresh fruit to your water pitcher and keep it in the refrigerator. Oranges, apples, lemons, limes, and strawberries all add flavor—and eye appeal—without adding many calories. Try combining fruits for even more variation.

One Potato, Two Potato

● Put fresh homemade french fries in a paper bag, add salt, and shake. Excess grease is absorbed by the paper, reducing the fat, and the fries are salted at the same time.

● For an even healthier version, here's how to make crispy steak-cut "fries." Slice potatoes into wedges and coat them lightly with nonstick cooking spray. Toss them in a bowl with cornflake crumbs and line up the potatoes on a cookie sheet. Bake at 400 degrees for 40 minutes, or until brown and crisp.

Soak up excess oil in homemade french fries by shaking them in a paper bag first.

● Slimmed-down mashed potatoes? You bet. Instead of adding milk or butter to the potatoes, use low-fat chicken broth. The potatoes whip up just as nicely, and no one will ever miss the fat.

Reducing Calories and Fat

● If you're dieting, you know how important portion control is, and you may also know that weighing your food is a good method of controlling the portions. Don't cheat: To make sure your kitchen measuring scale is accurate, place nine pennies on the scale—they should weigh exactly 1 ounce. If they don't, adjust the scale accordingly.

● Here's a low-cal version of guacamole dip: Dice half an avocado and add it to a bowl of salsa or picante sauce. Delicious.

● Baked foods are much healthier than fried. Bake fish wrapped in lettuce for a moist, tender, and delicious meal.

● Shave 16 calories from your hamburger by substituting a slice of tomato for the ketchup.

● Opt for white poultry meat over dark. White meat has fewer calories and about one-third less fat.

● To keep chicken moist when you bake it, don't remove the skin. Cook the chicken first, then remove the skin.

● Tomato juice makes a flavorful fat-free liquid for pot roast.

● To reduce fat and calories, grill tuna, swordfish, or salmon in place of beef when making shish kabobs. On the skewer, alternate fish cubes with decorative chunks of fresh or unsweetened pineapple.

● Take the meat out of lasagna and substitute spinach filling. Mix equal parts of low-fat cottage cheese and cooked, drained spinach. Spread the mixture over cooked lasagna noodles, cover with tomato sauce, and bake at 375 degrees for 45 minutes.

● Sauté vegetables in a nonstick skillet with a bit of low-fat chicken broth. Sauté a small amount at a time; if you overload the pan, the vegetables will steam.

Frozen Snacks

● Eat a frozen banana. Slice a very ripe banana, seal it in foil, and keep it in the freezer. Frozen banana is a palate pleaser with only about 100 calories.

● A dozen frozen grapes (40 calories) make another tasty treat.

● A glass of skim milk blended with some ripe fruit and crushed ice makes a frothy low-calorie shake. (For more options, see *One Hundred 100-Calorie Snacks,* pages 188–190.)

Just Desserts

● If you really need some chocolate (and who doesn't at some time or other?), opt for one or two pieces of chocolate-covered fruit, skim milk with chocolate syrup, or 10 to 15 chocolate-covered raisins.

● Drizzle some chocolate syrup on a slice of angel food cake or low-fat pound cake.

Diet-Friendly Dining Out

● Order an appetizer and a large salad for your meal.

● Eating at a restaurant that has a salad bar? Pile up your plate with

---

Size It Up

Need to size up a portion quickly, without benefit of a scale or measuring cup? Use this "handy" guide to help you visualize the proper portion.

Your thumb = 1 ounce cheese or meat

Your thumb tip = 1 tablespoon

Your fingertip = 1 teaspoon

Your cupped hand = 1 to 2 ounces pretzels

Your palm (minus fingers) = 2 to 3 ounces cooked meat

Your fist = ½ cup cooked rice or pasta
½ cup cooked peas or chopped veggies
½ cup chopped fruit
½ cup chopped nuts
½ cup ice cream or frozen yogurt

½ c.

---

veggies that come in large pieces— like carrot and celery sticks. The time it takes to eat these morsels gives your stomach time to feel that it's being satisfied. But proceed with care— prepared salads are usually smothered with mayonnaise or oily dressings. Instead, choose undressed veggies and sprinkle them with some lemon juice or balsamic vinegar.

● Or bring your own favorite low-calorie dressing to the restaurant. You can buy boxes of single-serving packets to tuck into your handbag.

● Wait 20 minutes before having a second helping. That is how long it takes for your brain to let your body know it's satiated.

● Take a salad-bar plate and ask to have your entrée served on it. Smaller plates make it clear that restaurant portions are really much too abundant.

● Mentally divide your plate into quarters: one quarter for protein, one quarter for carbohydrate, and one half for vegetables and fruits. This proportion usually represents about 500 calories for the meal.

Menu Talk

Knowing what these descriptive terms mean can help you choose diet-friendly fare.

FULL OF BUTTER, OIL, OR CHEESE	ALMOST FAT-FREE
✔ Alfredo (rich sauce of butter, cream, and Parmesan cheese)	✔ Au jus (cooked in natural juices)
✔ All'olio (in oil)	✔ Baked
✔ Au gratin (with cheese or bread crumbs)	✔ Blackened (rubbed with spicy flavorings, then cooked in a skillet)
✔ Béarnaise (sauce of vinegar, wine, tarragon, and shallots, reduced and blended with egg yolks and butter)	✔ Broiled
✔ Béchamel (thick sauce made of butter and flour mixed with milk)	✔ Grilled or grillé
✔ Beurre blanc ("white butter" sauce made by adding butter to reduction of vinegar, wine, and shallots)	✔ Marinara (tomato-based sauce)
	✔ Poached or poché
✔ Carbonara (sauce composed of cream, eggs, Parmesan cheese, and bits of bacon or ham)	✔ Primavera (with fresh vegetables)
	✔ Roasted or rôti
✔ Français, Francese (pan drippings with wine and butter added)	✔ Steamed
✔ Hollandaise (sauce made with butter and egg yolks)	
✔ Parmigiana (meat or vegetable topped with Parmesan and mozzarella cheeses and tomato slices)	
✔ Piccata (veal or chicken sautéed in butter, topped with lemon or parsley)	
✔ Scampi (fish or seafood brushed with oil or butter and then broiled)	

● Always opt to eat with chopsticks in an Asian restaurant. You'll eat more slowly, in smaller bites, so you'll be satiated sooner.

● Don't get sidelined by rich and tempting menu options. Call ahead of time and ask the restaurant about its low-fat, low-calorie options. Then stick to your plan when you get to the restaurant by not looking at the menu.

● You can have a glass of wine with dinner, but opt for a lower-calorie dry white wine spritzer.

● The rule of thumb for alcoholic beverages: The higher the proof, the higher the number of calories.

● Steer away from drinks made with fruit juices and milk bases. These increase the calorie count considerably.

● Skip the bread basket. Ask for a crudité plate if you need to munch.

Eat Right to Feel Good

● One good way to cut down on the fat in your diet is to eat less meat. Here are some nutritious staples of meatless cuisine. Add vegetables, a little oil or cheese, and then enjoy some flavors that may be unfamiliar.

BARLEY

● This grain has a mild, starchy flavor and slightly chewy texture. Use it as you would rice or as a hot cereal.

BULGUR

● Parboiled dried and cracked wheat, bulgur is quick to prepare and has a nutty flavor. Good hot or cold, bulgur is complemented by lemon; it's the basic ingredient of tabbouleh.

CORNMEAL

● Yellow, white, and, less commonly, blue corn kernels are ground in several grades to make cornmeal. Use in baked goods or to make polenta.

COUSCOUS

● A very small pasta made from semolina (a variety of wheat), couscous is often used in pilafs and spicy stews.

DRIED BEANS

● Beans are tasty and inexpensive. Many are available canned, which eliminates the otherwise lengthy soaking and cooking time. Add kidney beans, chickpeas, lentils, or black beans to salads or pasta, or mix beans with any grain for a complete protein.

MILLET

● A tiny round yellow grain with a slightly nutty flavor, millet is used like rice. You might find it surprising that it is a good substitute for pasta.

QUINOA

● This tiny grain has a smoky fragrance and a crunchy texture. Unlike most grains, it is a source of complete protein.

RICE

● There are many varieties of rice, each with a distinctive flavor. Look beyond basic white or brown to try jasmine, basmati, red, or other kinds. Knowing these terms will help you purchase smartly:

Brown rice retains its natural hull. It has a stronger flavor and chewier texture than white rice and takes a little longer to cook. Both long and short grain varieties are available.

White rice is brown rice that has been polished. It is usually enriched.

Converted rice is white rice that has been parboiled and dried; it cooks fairly quickly.

Arborio rice is a type of white rice that stays firm when cooked. It is the classic rice used for risotto.

TOFU

● Sometimes called bean curd, tofu is made from soybean milk. *Soft* tofu is smooth and creamy. Use it for whipping, blending, and crumbling to make dips and dressings. *Firm* tofu is good for slicing and cubing to use in stir-fries, soups, and casseroles.

WHEAT BERRIES

● Crunchy, flavorful whole wheat grains are excellent in hot or cold dishes. Use as you would rice.

WILD RICE

● Not truly a variety of rice, wild rice is a kind of grass. The seeds are long, dark, and full of flavor.

Foreign Intrigue

Ethnic restaurants offer a wide range of diet-savvy choices—and weighty ones as well. Here's how to make the best choices from three of the most popular international cuisines.

	GOOD CHOICES	FAT TRAPS	TIPS
CHINESE	Broth-based vegetable soups; chop suey or chow mein; steamed or stir-fried dishes; steamed dumplings	Breaded, battered, crispy, fried, or sweet-and-sour entrées; cashew or peanut dishes; egg or spring rolls; fried rice; lo mein; Peking duck; spareribs; lobster and other premade sauces	● Request that stir-fries be made with minimal oil. ● Stretch 1 cup of a high-fat dish with steamed rice. ● For a filling meal, order steamed chicken or seafood with veggies, brown rice, and sauce on the side.
ITALIAN	Baked, broiled, or grilled chicken, seafood, or meat; pasta (with marinara or other noncreamy sauces); polenta; vinaigrette dishes	Antipasto platters; baked stuffed clams; cream sauces; eggplant (grilled, baked, or fried—it soaks up oil); meatballs; prosciutto (ham); stuffed pastas such as ravioli or tortellini	● Check how dishes are prepared; are the veggies in pasta primavera, for example, sautéed or steamed? ● Not all tomato sauces are low in fat; those described as "pink" are usually made with cream.
MEXICAN	Baked burritos; black beans; fajitas; gazpacho; salsa; grilled seafood or chicken; seviche; soft tortillas	Chili con queso; chimichangas; enchiladas; guacamole; nachos; quesadillas; refried beans; sopaipillas (fried dough); tacos	● Ask the waiter to bring warm tortillas (not tortilla chips) to the table for munching. ● Shun high-fat add-ons like sour cream and shredded cheese, but help yourself to salsa—almost no calories!

The Right Moves

Eating right is only half of what it takes to trim pounds and inches. In order to get the figure you want, you have to get going.

● For the ultimate in exercise motivation, instead of investing in an exercise leotard, wear your bathing suit with tights when you exercise, and work out in front of a mirror. You can't help but work out that much harder.

● Never again watch television without exercising. Walk on a treadmill, ride a stationary bicycle, or do leg lifts, stomach crunches, and arm curls.

● Put your time on a stationary bike or treadmill to double use. Borrow books on tape from your library and listen while you work out: fiction, self-help, and language tapes are ideal.

● Another mind-expanding, body-shrinking option: Listen to or watch travel tapes as you walk on the treadmill or ride a stationary bike. You'll feel as though you're actually going somewhere.

● If you drive to a gym, always park your car as far away as possible so you can walk those extra steps to warm up before your workout and cool down afterward.

● No need to invest in an expensive stair stepper if you take the stairs, rather than the elevator or escalator, whenever you can.

● Fresh air and exercise are good for everyone in your family. Walk or jog alongside your kids as they bike or skate — or join them.

● One day a week, retire your car keys. Walk or bike to wherever you need to go. You'll be getting your exercise and saving money on gas at the same time.

● Walk the dog. If you don't have one, offer to walk your neighbor's dog.

Banish bathing-suit blues by exercising in your swim togs.

Everyday Exercise

According to a report from the U.S. Surgeon General, burning off just 150 extra calories a day is all it takes to reap the health benefits of exercise. These everyday activities can help you fritter off the fat.

✔ Washing and waxing a car for 45 to 60 minutes

✔ Scrubbing floors or windows for 45 to 60 minutes

✔ Bicycling 5 miles in 30 minutes

✔ Gardening for 30 to 45 minutes

✔ Fast social dancing for 30 minutes

✔ Pushing a stroller 1½ miles in 30 minutes

✔ Raking leaves for 30 minutes

✔ Shoveling snow for 15 minutes

One Hundred 100-Calorie Snacks

Sometimes you just can't quash the urge to nosh. Below is a list of "safe" snacks. If you keep these foods on hand, you won't be caught unarmed the next time a snack attack hits.

CHOCOLATEY	CALORIES
Chocolate-covered banana (½ medium dipped in 1 teaspoon fat-free chocolate syrup and frozen)	61
Chocolate-covered graham cracker (1)	68
Chocolate-covered raisins (14)	65
Chocolate-covered strawberries (1 cup dipped in 1 ounce fat-free chocolate syrup)	86
Chocolate-flavored coffee (6 ounces)	6
Chocolate jelly beans (¾ ounce)	78
Chocolate milk, 1% fat (5 ounces)	89
Fat-free chocolate-chip cookies (3)	86
Nonfat hot chocolate (6 ounces)	50

CREAMY	CALORIES
Artificially sweetened nonfat French vanilla yogurt	100
Banana (½ medium)	53
Cheese melt (½ toasted English muffin broiled with ½ ounce nonfat Cheddar cheese)	90
Cinnamon-melt toast (1 thin slice low-calorie white bread spread with 1 teaspoon part-skim ricotta cheese, sprinkled with sugar and cinnamon, and popped under broiler)	72
Fat-free cream cheese (1 tablespoon) with celery	21
Fat-free pudding, 70% skim milk (1 cup)	100
Goat cheese (1 tablespoon) on 2 slices Melba toast	80
Mozzarella (1 ounce part skim)	72
Peanut butter (1 teaspoon) on 1 graham cracker	91

CRUNCHY	CALORIES
Animal crackers (5)	51
Apple	81
Asparagus (raw, 6 medium stalks)*	20
Biscotti (plain, 1)	90
Breadsticks (2)	83
Broccoli (raw, ½ cup florets)*	6
Cabbage (raw, 1 cup shredded)	20
Carrot (raw, 1 medium)*	31
Cauliflower (raw, 1 cup)*	24
Celery (raw, 3 stalks)*	18
Cucumber (1 cup sliced florets)*	14
Fat-free cheese puffs (1 ounce)	100
Melba toast (5 pieces)	100
Mini rice cakes (½ ounce)	60
Pepper (sweet, raw, 1 cup sliced)*	27
Popcorn (air-popped, 2 cups), sprinkled with 2 teaspoons grated Parmesan cheese	80
Pumpernickel toast (1 slice)	80
Tortilla chips (baked, 1 cup) with 2 tablespoons salsa	98
* dipped in ½ cup nonfat plain yogurt seasoned with dill or curry	+68

REFRESHING

	CALORIES
Fat-free (97%) ice cream (½ cup)	100
Frozen fruit-juice bar	63
Frozen nonfat yogurt (½ cup)	100
Fruit sorbet (½ cup)	70
Grapes (frozen, ¾ cup)	85
Italian ice (1 cup)	100
Melon balls (frozen, 1 cup) with squirt of lime juice and drizzle of honey	92
Orange cup (½ cup juice from concentrate), frozen in paper cup	55
Pineapple chunks (packed in juice, ½ cup), frozen and partially thawed, with 1 sliced dried date and sprinkled with cinnamon	63
Watermelon (1 cup cubes)	50

SALTY

	CALORIES
Chicken broth, instant (1 cup)	21
Dill pickle (1 large)	12
Fat-free potato chips (1 ounce)	100
Feta cheese (½ ounce) and 1 medium peach	88
Olives (10)	52
Pretzels (¾ ounce)	83
Saltines (2)	26
Tomato juice (¾ cup)	30

STARCHY

	CALORIES
Baked potato (medium), topped with 2 tablespoons nonfat sour cream	99
Cooked beans, any variety (¼ cup)	95
Cooked cream of rice cereal (¾ cup)	60
Cooked enriched pasta (½ cup)	98
Fat-free crackers, whole wheat (5)	50
Gingerbread (2-inch-square piece)	88
Mini bagel	70
Mini doughnut (cake style, with powdered sugar)	50
Sweet potato (medium, baked)	59
Vanilla wafers (3)	59
Waffle (frozen, 1)	92
Whole-grain bread (1 slice)	90

SWEET

	CALORIES
Applesauce (unsweetened, 1 cup), sprinkled with cinnamon	100
Bagel (½ of 2-ounce bagel), spread with 2 teaspoons nonfat cream cheese and 1 teaspoon all-fruit preserves	100
Butterscotch candy (¾ ounce)	84
Chutney roll-up (1 ounce roasted white-meat turkey with 1 tablespoon chutney rolled in a lettuce leaf)	73
Dates (4 dried)	92
Fat-free fig bar (1 cookie)	68
Fat-free toaster pastry (½ pastry)	83
Fig (fresh, 1 medium)	37
Flavored herbal tea (6 ounces)	2
Fruit gelatin (sugar-free, ½ cup) with 2 tablespoons reduced-calorie whipped topping	28
Gingersnaps (2)	58

SWEET, continued	CALORIES
Gumdrops (7)	95
Hard candies (½ ounce)	55
Ice milk, vanilla (⅓ cup)	90
Jelly beans (½ ounce)	78
Ladyfingers (2)	79
Lemon drops (½ ounce)	53
Licorice (½ ounce)	61
Marshmallow (1 large)	23
Oatmeal raisin cookie (1 medium)	60
Papaya (½ medium)	59
Pear (1 medium)	98
Raisins (3 tablespoons)	93
Raspberries (fresh, 1 cup), mixed with blueberries (fresh, ½ cup)	100
Sugar wafers (2)	35

TART/JUICY	CALORIES
Apple butter (1 tablespoon)	32
Apricots (3 medium)	50
Cantaloupe (1 cup pieces)	57
Fruit cocktail (packed in juice, ½ cup)	56
Grapefruit (½ medium)	37
Honeydew melon (½ cup cubes/balls)	30
Kiwifruit (1 medium)	46
Plum (1 medium)	36
Tangerine (1 medium)	37

Label Lowdown

Understanding food package labels can help you make healthier choices.

Low Fat
Three grams of fat or less per serving. The food must also have 3 grams fat or less per 100 grams.

Light, Lite
One-third fewer calories than a comparable product. Other senses of "light"—for color, taste, or smell—must be clearly explained.

(Numeral)% Fat-Free
The food is truly low in fat.

Low Calorie
Fewer than 40 calories per serving and per 100 grams.

A Source of (Nutrient)
Per serving, such a food must provide 10% to 19% of the daily quota for the stated nutrient.

Low Sodium
Contains less than 140 milligrams per serving and per 100 grams. Foods claiming to be sodium-free or salt-free must contain less than 5 milligrams of sodium per serving.

(Nutrient)-Free
Contains a nutritionally trivial amount of the named nutrient.

Cholesterol-Free
Less than 2 milligrams of cholesterol and 2 grams or less of saturated fat per serving. Foods that never contain cholesterol must underscore that fact if they choose to make the claim.

High in (Nutrient)
One serving must provide 20% or more of the recommended daily intake for that nutrient. In the case of fiber, the label must declare the total fat content if a serving also packs more than 3 grams of fat.

CHAPTER 15

Family Fun!

Don't just eat—dine! Little touches like candles and linens make everyday dinners special.

Now that your papers are tamed, your closets are a work of art, and breakfast and dinners practically prepare themselves, what are you going to do with all that free time? We've got more than a few fun-filled ideas.

Celebrate!

● When's the last time you bought or baked a birthday cake . . . and it wasn't anybody's birthday? Go ahead, splurge, with candles, confetti, the works. It's amazing how much goodwill one little birthday cake can generate.

● Don't let those party clothes languish in the closet until the next special occasion arises. Designate a "Dress-Up-for-Dinner" night. Set out the good china and silver, light the candles, and treat yourself and your family to an elegant feast. Even put on elegant airs. It's fun to be someone else for an evening.

● Learn about and celebrate another culture's holiday. Prepare a Mexican meal for Cinco de Mayo; make potato latkes and play dreidl games to celebrate Hanukkah; participate in a St. Patrick's Day parade. Not only is this fun, but it also helps broaden everyone's understanding of other cultures.

● Remember to acknowledge life's little accomplishments— your son learned to tie his shoes, your daughter knows all of the multiplication tables, your husband broke 100 on the golf course, you ran a mile. These are everyday triumphs that can be rewarded with a card, a flower, a pin that says, "Good Job!" It's a

way to elevate self-esteem and encourage everyone to share in another's success.

● Throw a party for someone who doesn't ordinarily get a lot of attention. A widowed neighbor, for example, or someone in a nearby nursing home. Bringing joy into someone else's life can be very rewarding.

Game Plan

● Turn off the TV, dust off an old board game, and play with your family. You'd be surprised how much fun you can glean from a game of Clue, Monopoly, or Pictionary. And if it's been a while since you've played with your children, you'll see how much their game-playing skills have progressed.

Turn off the TV and let the games (and good times) begin.

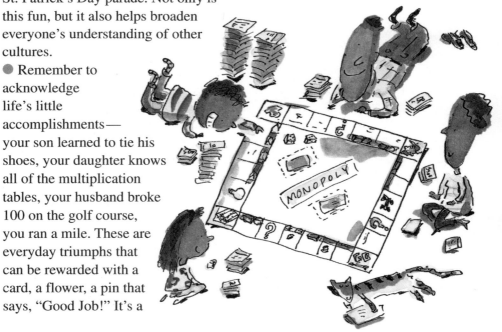

Integrate a regular "Sports Night" into your schedule. Your family or even friends might want to join the fun. Gather the softball equipment and head for the park. Go to a bowling alley and play a game or two.

Organize a "Field Day" at home, with relay, sack, and wheelbarrow races. Put the kids in charge of picking the events and gathering the equipment. Most of them are well versed in these kinds of games.

Dig out a deck of cards and learn to play a new card game.

Garage sales and thrift stores are terrific places to buy different games for very little money. Maybe you can even do a trade—bring an old game that's played out and swap it for something different. Friends are another good source to tap when it comes to finding something new. Offer to trade with them too.

Puzzles—large ones with lots of little pieces—can keep a family occupied for days. Place one on a large piece of cardboard or puzzle mat so you can move it out of the way when you're not actively working on it.

Take out a book of mind games, riddles, or 5-minute mysteries and take turns trying to solve them.

Support a local sports team and attend the games with your friends or family.

A Little Night Music

Do you or other members of your family play musical instruments? Why not have a regular concert evening? Pick a piece of music that you can play together, learn it, rehearse it, then perform it for yourselves and perhaps even some friends.

Have a family sing-along. Pick a theme: Broadway show tunes, Beatles' songs, sixties folk songs, or spirituals. Play a tape or records the week preceding your song fest so that everyone can learn the words.

Take in a concert at a local high school, college, or music school. If you're lucky enough to live in an area with a full-fledged orchestra, see if they offer discount tickets to families. Sometimes you can even arrange to sit in on a rehearsal. Investigate local chamber music groups or instrument-specific bands.

In the summer, check local listings for town offerings of open-air musical events. Make an evening of it by bringing along a picnic dinner, blankets, and chairs. Don't forget the bug spray.

The Play's the Thing

You don't have to pay a fortune to reap the rewards of a theatrical experience. Look up listings for local theater companies and high school, college, or community theaters. The offerings usually range from children's theater to off-Broadway quality productions. With a little investigation, you can find something you'll all enjoy watching together.

Take part in a production. Family members can try out for different parts or join the stage crew—build sets, paint scenery, sew costumes, help with makeup and wardrobe. Younger children can hand out programs on opening night, and everyone will enjoy going to the cast party afterward.

● Put on a play at home. Recruit friends and neighbors to play roles or to become part of the viewing audience.

● Host a murder-mystery evening. You can buy a kit or borrow one from your local library. These kits include character assignments, clues, costume, and prop ideas.

● Attend a poetry reading. Large bookstores and colleges are the best places to check for these types of events. Best of all, they're usually free.

● Is there a television studio nearby? Write away for tickets (they are usually free) and become part of the studio audience. Good family-friendly options are game shows, sitcoms, and magic shows.

Garden Party

● Does your community have a garden plot you can work for a season? There's something for everyone to do: digging and turning the soil, mixing in organic ingredients, choosing which vegetables and flowers to plant, watering, weeding, and ultimately, harvesting. You all get fresh air, exercise, an understanding of how nature works, and maybe a great big salad or delicious vegetable stir-fry to enjoy as you reap the rewards of your hard work.

● Beautify your town together. Check with the town hall about which community gardens need volunteers.

Whodunit? That's for you to know and the kids to find out.

Every time you drive by that particular public lot and see it start to blossom, you'll feel a sense of family pride.

Fit for Families

● When's the last time you all took a walk together? Very often we're so busy scurrying from one place to another by car, we never stop to admire the beauty that's within walking distance of our homes. Get into the habit of regular after-dinner walks. It's a good way to get some exercise and become reacquainted with each other and the neighborhood.

● Participate in different races together. Don't plan on breaking any records. Just sign up as a family and have fun. Very often you can get some exercise and support a worthy cause as well. And many "races" offer a walk/ride option to participants.

● Join your local YMCA or other affordable family health club. Many of them offer separate classes for different age groups, as well as family fitness clinics.

● Bicycling is another family-friendly activity. If your youngster is too small to ride a bike, get a bicycle seat or an approved "baby trailer" to attach to your bike. You can explore local parks, small streets, and neighborhoods while benefiting from the fresh air and exercise at the same time.

● Learn or relearn to skate. Most communities and cities have an ice-skating rink nearby, some run by the town. For a small fee, you and your kids can spend an afternoon gliding on the ice (or trying to). If it's been years since you donned a pair of skates, let your kids be your teachers. They get a kick out of being "in charge" and showing you how to get up again after you take a spill.

● Roller or in-line skating is another fun activity that everyone can enjoy, and it doesn't have to be confined to a rink. Just remember to wear the appropriate safety equipment— helmets, knee and wrist pads—and observe the rules of the road.

Saturday Night at the Movies

● Treat yourself to a night at the movies—at home. Rent or borrow a video that everyone in your family can watch. Serve popcorn and soda, even spring for those great big boxes of Milk Duds or Raisinettes if that's your thing. Turn the lights down, settle in, and enjoy the show.

● Can't find a video that everyone wants to watch from among the latest releases? Go classic. Look on the shelves for old musicals, comedies, or even reruns of classic television shows. They may be old to you, but they're new to your kids. And they'll get a sampling of the kinds of things you watched as a kid.

● Here's a way to give an old, familiar movie a new spin: Pop it in the VCR but turn off the sound. Now take turns talking for each of the characters, making up the dialog as you go along. Since you've probably all seen the movie many times before, you know what the action's going to be. Hilarious!

● Dig out those old family movies (you may have to rent an old-style reel-to-reel projector and screen) and project them for your kids. They love to see how you looked as a kid, and you'll get the opportunity to explain who's who among long-lost relatives. You might even catch a glimpse of Grandma's house 30 or 40 years ago. Have your kids pick out landmarks and explain how different things look now.

● Make a movie. If that video camera doesn't get much use, recharge the battery and put it to work. Choose a director, a screenwriter, and actors for your homemade flick, and spend a day or two producing it. Invite friends to the "premiere." If this seems too ambitious, create a commercial advertising toothpaste, new fashions, or a favorite product.

Dance, Dance, Dance

● Check with a local dance studio to see if they offer classes on specialty dancing: ballroom or hip-hop, swing or square dancing. You might get some resistance at first, but once you all attend the class, you'll be pleasantly surprised by your family's enthusiasm.

● If you really do have two left feet, you can still enjoy a dance experience. Attend a performance of a local dance company or a recital at a nearby studio or college. A lot of effort and attention goes into these performances, and tickets are far less expensive than those for professional troupes.

● Do you have a large, finished basement or family room, or do you have access to one? Together with some other families, rent a jukebox and throw a fifties-style party, complete

Don't just sit there! You could be dancing—and having a great time too.

with poodle skirts, ponytails (ducktails for the boys), and ice cream sodas. If someone among the group knows how to do any dances of the fifties era, have him or her teach the rest.

● Square dancing is especially fun for families. You don't need any special skill to do it, and if you master just a few basic moves (which most children learn in school) and follow the caller's instructions, you can have a ball. Check out your local newspaper's listings for country or country-western dancing events. If you know of enough people who are interested, chip in to hire a caller and a hall and have a square-dancing party yourself.

● Teach your kids the dances that were popular in "your day" and have them teach you the moves they do today. If Grandma and Grandpa are around, ask them to join in. Switch back and forth, trading your music for theirs, or dance to their music your way and vice versa.

Historical Society

Nothing brings families together faster than a genealogical search. Trace your family tree back as far as you can go.

● Have your kids participate in the interviewing and information-gathering process. Start with relatives who live nearby, asking such questions as who came from where and when did they move there, then expand the search to include distant relatives and cousins. Your kids will love to learn about their family history. Your local library or town hall can help you get started with

Family facts can be fascinating. Let kids search for their roots.

a "trace-your-family-roots" kit. There are also excellent software programs you can buy for your computer to guide you through the process. And if you have access to the Internet, it's easy to go global with your search. Who knows? You may connect with some long-lost relative, unearth a family secret, or uncover a branch of the family you never knew existed.

● Start a family news chain. To begin, contact family members to see who wants to participate and list them in alphabetical order. Have everyone in your immediate family contribute to a letter, then pass it on to the next person on the list. They'll add to the letter and send it on. In four to eight weeks, everyone participating will have received a packet of news. When the letter has been passed all around and returns to you, replace the news you had contributed before and start the circle again.

● Interview each other for a family newsletter or radio program. Ask off-beat questions. The answers may surprise you.

● Learn some of the customs and phrases of your family's countries of origin. We are a nation of immigrants, yet many second-, third-, and fourth-generation families have lost much of their rich foreign heritage through the assimilation process. Ask Grandma and Great-Grandma for their old family recipes and prepare them at a special family dinner at which they're the guests of honor.

● Pull out all the old family photos and introduce your children to long-gone friends and relatives. Look for resemblances among the ancestors, and encourage your kids to ask questions about who they were, what they did, and how they're related.

● Take a Saturday or weekend trip to the "old neighborhood" if it's within driving distance. Show the kids the house where you grew up, the field where you played ball, and the school you went to. If the old house is still standing, knock on the door and explain to the current residents who

you are and ask if they would mind if you showed your kids around. You'd be surprised how accommodating most people will be, and you may even find the beam in the attic where you carved your name a long time ago.

● Look up old friends and relatives you haven't seen or spent time with for a very long time and plan a family outing together. Children love to hear stories from way back when. And since these are the people who were a part of your formative years, your children may gain a better understanding of who you are as well.

● Pick an era you'd like to have been a part of—ancient Greece, colonial times, the Roaring Twenties—and try to live that way for just one day. Everyone in the family can take part in researching what was—and wasn't—around during that time period. Consider what to wear, eat, even what games to play after dinner.

● Do you have a historical village near your home? Pay a visit to get a

Getting involved in a charitable effort can promote personal growth and family closeness.

FEED The SMITH FAMILY BAKE SALE

Lemonade 25¢ a glass

25¢ a slice

real sense of what life was like at another point in time. Some of the villages schedule old-time baseball games, candlelight walks during the holidays, and Sunday services. If history really intrigues your family, ask about becoming a volunteer so that you, too, can dress in period costume and give tours.

Activate Activism

● Does your community lack a playground? Have an unsightly lot that needs cleaning up? Teach your kids how to effect change—and improve the community you live in at the same time. Discuss what you, as a family, can do to make a difference. Then go to town hall to learn what the procedures are, and assign everyone a task according to age and ability. Older children might like to start collecting names for a petition; younger ones can make signs and posters.

● Pick a cause or charity that's near and dear to your heart and rally the family round to do some fund-raising. Host a bake sale or car wash; organize a backyard carnival. Collect cans for a local soup kitchen; organize a clothing drive for a homeless shelter or perhaps for a family left homeless by a fire or natural disaster.

● Get involved in the electoral campaign of a politician or in the activities of a cause you believe in. Let the kids fold mailers, stuff mailboxes (with you beside them, of course), or go door to door with you to collect signatures. This is a firsthand lesson in civics that'll stay with them their whole lives.

● Ask your local church or synagogue what you can do as a family to help someone in need. Perhaps it's prepare and deliver a meal or provide babysitting services, house repairs, or lawn work. It may not sound like everyone's definition of "fun," but then again, doing good offers its own brand of rewards.

Local Attractions

● Get on the mailing list for colleges and universities in your area and attend lectures, debates, and other events that are of interest to your family. Because these events are subsidized by the schools, the costs are usually quite reasonable. And students either get a greater discount or can attend for free.

● Look in the paper for art gallery openings and shows. Attend those that are appropriate for families. (If you're unsure about a show's content, call the gallery and ask.)

● Write or call a local radio station and ask if it allows audience members to attend a broadcast. Choose a broadcast based on your interests (talk, music, sports). Tickets are usually free.

● Do you live near a county or state fairground, or a horse show ground? If you arrive early in the morning, you can watch the exhibitors groom, feed, or exercise their animals—or watch trained animals practice their routines.

Have you ever wondered how sneakers are made? Boats or cars assembled? Candy wrapped? If there's a manufacturing facility near your town, go on a tour! It's interesting to see how things get made. The tours are usually family friendly, not too expensive, and are often capped off with a free "sample" of the product. And there's often a factory store.

If manufacturing isn't your thing, perhaps you could visit a farm in your area. Write or call to make arrangements to take a tour, even ask if your family can participate for a day. Most children love animals, and farms are usually very "hands-on" places where they can feed and pet them. Vegetable farms and orchards often have "pick-your-own" harvests.

5 Fun Things to Do on a Saturday Night

Play a Card or Board Game
Gather 'round the kitchen table for a rousing, old-fashioned game such as Go Fish, checkers, or Scrabble. Have a funny "award"—a ribbon or crown—that is passed to each new winner.

Go Play
After supper, go to the local playground and play! Don't just sit on the sidelines while your kids have all the fun. Get on the swing and challenge them to a how-high-can-you-go contest; share a teeter-totter (you may need to offset the balance to make it work!). Treat everyone to an ice cream sundae afterward.

Switch Places
Create an "alternate universe" and switch roles: Kids be the adults, adults be the kids. Let the children plan and prepare dinner, choose the after-supper entertainment (within reason, of course), and put you to bed first. Just remember to establish some overall ground rules for what children are and aren't allowed to do in their "adult" mode.

Role Play
Try this guessing game for an evening of fun: Everyone in the family pretends to be someone else. It can be a movie or television personality, a character from a book, even a cartoon character. Give subtle clues about who you are by what you do, choose to eat, even wear for the night. Everyone takes turns guessing each other's identity.

Window Shop
Go shopping for something expensive—a new car, for example—that you have no intention of buying. Make sure everyone's clear that this is just a pretend shopping trip and make the most of it. (Tell your kids not to reveal the game to the salespeople.)

CHAPTER 16

Tips on Trips

Where do you want to go? Your dream vacation may be within your reach.

Whether you're relaxing at the shore for the weekend or taking a month-long trek across the country, the best vacation starts before you leave the house. Wherever you decide to go, we'll help you find the best bargains so your vacation dollars go the distance—and then some. We also include hints to help you decide where to go, what to do, and how to plan, pack, budget, and more. So get out your guidebooks, pick a destination, and go!

What's the Dream?

Remember, include everyone in the planning phase, from selecting a destination to deciding what to do once you get there.

WHERE TO?

● First, decide what kind of vacation you want to take. Do you want to go to a city and visit museums, take in theater, and enjoy other cultural offerings? Or is an adventure vacation more your speed—canoeing down a river, hiking in a national park, or biking from inn to inn? Maybe pure pleasure is what you're after—at an all-inclusive resort or spa, or on a luxury cruise. If you crave a break from civilization, perhaps camping, RVing, or staying in a cabin is right for you.

The world's a smaller place, thanks to the Internet.

COST IT OUT

● Next, determine your vacation budget. The amount you can spend will greatly affect the outcome of your where-to-go, what-to-do decision. Be sure to account for the following:

Transportation Calculate not only what it will cost to get there but also the cost of transportation once you arrive—that is, for rental car, buses, taxis, trains, and such. Remember to include gas and tolls in your estimates.

Where you'll stay Hotel, motel, condo, house swap, cabin . . . know what your vacation expectations are—what creature comforts you *must* have—to make your stay enjoyable (share a bathroom, never!) and how much you're willing to spend for them.

Admission fees If a theme park is the centerpiece of your vacation plans, be aware that the costs can add up. Figure in entrance fees, meals on site, and extras at the outset so you won't feel overwhelmed by expenses when you arrive. Often travel package deals offer the best rates.

Babysitting/children's programs If you're hoping to spend a little time without the kids on your vacation, factor in the costs of their care or entertainment.

Extras Gifts, souvenirs, tips, and film processing: Account for these costs up front and you won't get caught short.

Smart Planning

● Once you've selected a site, let the kids do some research to find out what local attractions your vacation destination offers. Encourage them to look through books and brochures and to make a priority list of their must-do's. Combine the lists into one, making sure that everyone's No. 1 and No. 2 choices are on it.

● The Internet is a great source of travel information, from where to stay to what to do when you get there. (See *Travel Bargains Online,* page 207.) You can e-mail the chamber of commerce of the city you're visiting, describe the kinds of activities you'd like to participate in, and ask them to send you brochures. Sometimes it's worth booking certain excursions in advance so you don't risk being shut out when you get there.

Don't take a chance: Book excursions in advance.

● Talk to people who've been where you're going. Ask them very specific questions about how to get around, what attractions they liked best—and why—how much things cost, and if they would do things differently if they were to go again.

● Set aside enough time in advance to make reservations, send advance payments, and receive confirming documents or vouchers. Last-minute arrangements often fall prey to mix-ups and unconfirmed bookings. Always ask for your reservation number and confirmation by mail and check them for accuracy when you receive them. Bring the documents with you when you travel, just in case there's any discrepancy with your booking.

● Make sure you understand all the terms that apply to your booking, especially the cancellation penalties and refund policy.

● When traveling outside the United States, make photocopies of your passports and carry them separately. If you're using traveler's checks, make photocopies of them as well. Also make a list of your credit-card numbers. These precautions will make your trip a lot easier if you need to report or replace a lost or stolen document.

Vacation Budget Stretchers

Ask smart questions when you plan and book your travel arrangements— you'll save a significant amount of money. Here are some pointers:

AIRLINES

● Flying at odd hours may be worth losing some beauty sleep over, so ask the airline before you book. For a family of four, the savings could be considerable.

● If you are flying to or from a city with two or more airports nearby, such as New York (JFK, LaGuardia, Newark), San Francisco (Oakland, San Francisco International), or Chicago (Midway, O'Hare), there may be fare differentials from airport to airport— as much as $300 for a family of four. The cost difference may mean a longer drive to a more distant airport, but then again, the dollar savings may make the detour worth your while.

● Call late at night to get those as-advertised cheap seats. The cut-rate fares you often see advertised require a 14- or 21-day advance purchase or a Saturday night stay-over. There may be other restrictions buried in the small print, or there may be only one seat available at the advertised price. Here's something you can do: Try calling the airline's reservation number just after midnight. That's when the computers automatically cancel all low-cost reservations for which payment hasn't been made—freeing up some discount seats. Just be sure to call after midnight the airline's time—eastern time for Delta, for example, and central time for American and United.

● Consider taking a charter flight. Tour operators charge less for each seat than commercial airlines. If you can be flexible, this no-frills way of traveling can save you hundreds.

● If a flight is full, try calling the airline again at the beginning of a week. Cancellations tend to occur over the weekend or first thing Monday morning.

● Ticket consolidators can also offer you deep discounts on airfares. Here's how they work: Ticket consolidators buy tickets in bulk from airlines and resell them to the public at bargain prices. Try calling a consolidator if you're making last-minute travel plans and can't take advantage of 14- and 21-day advance-purchase deals. The

All aboard! Careful planning can make the journey enjoyable.

trade-offs? You might not have a choice of airlines and you won't be able to accrue frequent flier miles. You can usually find ads from ticket consolidators in the travel section of your hometown newspaper.

HOTELS

● When booking hotel rooms, always ask for the discounted rate. If you call the hotel's reservation desk, you'll most likely be quoted the "rack rate," the full price. Savvy travelers never pay rack rate. Ask about packages, specials, breakfast coupons, card-member privileges. Also inquire about the following hidden hotel costs:

Parking fees Usually included in the room fee, but ask to be sure.

Maximum room occupancy Some hotels/motels charge a per-room rate at no extra cost. Others have a per-person rate based on double occupancy— which means you may have to pay extra for kids.

Hotel occupancy fee This can add 5 to 15 percent to your room rate and is not always quoted by the reservation clerk, so be sure to ask.

CAR RENTALS

● Join a frequent flier program, even if you aren't one! Most commercial airline companies have relationships with car rental companies that give frequent flier members up to 30 percent off regular rates. When making your car reservations, ask, "What are your frequent flier discounts?" Members of credit unions, AARP, and other associations may also qualify for car rental discounts.

● Like airlines and hotels, car rental companies also offer special and promotional packages. Always ask about discounts, reduced rates for seniors, or other discounts. It's usually less expensive to keep a car weekly than on a day-by-day basis.

● Make rental arrangements on a per-day, free-mileage basis rather than a per-mile rate. These charges can really add up, and it's wise not to use a car rental company that offers only mileage rates.

● Additional insurance coverage can add an extra $7 to $10 per day, and you may not need it. Call your car insurance provider to find out what damages, losses, and injuries your policy covers for rental cars. If you're completely covered, simply decline the waiver. Also check with your credit-card companies to see if they provide coverage and what kind they offer. Some might pay for damages—with a high deductible—but won't cover personal injury.

● Be aware of drop-off fees. Driving from one destination to another is a great way to see the sights, but a drop-off charge (not returning the car to the same place you rented it from) could tag another $50 to $100 onto the cost. Plan a circular itinerary if you can.

● Return the car with a full tank of gas. It's far less expensive to fill the tank at a local station before returning the car than to have the car rental company put in the gas. They will charge you a refueling fee and a premium price for the gas itself.

CRUISES

● When you are considering a cruise, it always pays to ask about discounts. Even if you're booking early, ask your travel agent or the cruise line reservationist about discounted cabins. And if you don't mind making last-minute arrangements, you can often reap big savings. Up to a few days before the ship sets sail, cruise lines will try to fill empty cabins. Savings could run as much as 40 to 70 percent of normal prices. You will have to make arrangements to arrive at the departure city on time, however, which may mean a costly last-minute airfare.

The money you save on the cruise may not be worth the price you'd have to pay for the airline tickets.

● Since cruise companies are trying to attract families, children often travel free. Shop around for the best deal. You may have to pay only for the airfare for your children and a small activities fee. Everything else is included.

● Always expect the unexpected. Bad weather, for example, can derail a lot of plans—boating, swimming, skiing. Have a rainy-day option at the ready—a museum tour or souvenir shopping, for example—so the day won't seem like a loss.

Tips by Country

Although a tip is still a gratuity for good service, in many countries it's included directly in the bill. This guide should keep you from causing an international incident when you eat out in the world.

COUNTRY	TIP	COMMENT
France	12–15%	Usually included in hotel, restaurant bills.
Germany	10–15%	Service charge usually included in restaurant bill; small additional tip is norm.
Hong Kong	10–15%	Tipping common for all services.
Indonesia	10%	Usually included in bill; additional tip sometimes added.
Italy	10%	Tips expected for most services.
Japan	10–12%	Tip usually included in hotel, restaurant bills; otherwise tipping not common.
Malaysia	10%	Tipping usual for porters and room service.
Mexico	10%	Tipping common for most services.
U.K.	10–12%	Service charge usually included in restaurant bill.
U.S.	15–20%	Expected.

Travel Bargains Online

Travel Web sites can save you time and money. Take a look at the following to explore your destination in advance and to find the best deals.

VIRTUAL GUIDEBOOKS

Peruse dozens of travel books online— for free! Print out only the sections you want to take with you for a lighter carry-on.

Arthur Frommer's Budget Travel Online
www.frommers.com

Budget-travel guru Frommer has an information-packed site with an accent on bargains.

Fodor's Travel Online
www.fodorstravel.com

The Personal Budget Trip Planner lets you create your own guide to dozens of cities, with custom listings of hotels, restaurants, and sights.

Lonely Planet
www.lonelyplanet.com

You'll find details on sights around the globe plus a terrific photo gallery on this Web site.

Excite Travel
www.excite.com/travel

Here you'll get the the lowdown on hundreds of cities worldwide. After you select a city you'll see Fact Sheets that include such info as a city's seasonal temperatures and sales- and room-tax rates.

GETTING THERE, VIA THE WEB

Transportation can be the trickiest and most expensive part of any vacation. These sites will help you research options and can most likely help you save money.

American Automobile Association
www.aaa.com

Triple A offers free roadwork advisories and weather reports; $55 annual membership nets you discounts on hotels, restaurants, and theme park admissions.

MapQuest
www.mapquest.com

To receive routes for free, just type in your destination and print out the map and itinerary.

Amtrak
www.amtrak.com

Discounts for Amtrak are offered to students, seniors, and kids.

RailPass Express
www.railpass.com

Here you can find a dozen special fares and discounts for traveling Europe by train.

LOW-FARE SEARCH ENGINES

Once you get accustomed to using these three sites, you'll find them worth the effort. You'll have to register with a working e-mail address to use them, but they are pretty good at locating bargain airfare, hotel, and car-rental rates.

Preview Travel
www.previewtravel.com

Although it can be slow, Preview Travel lets you choose the flights you want, then alerts you to money-saving options for the same route.

Travelocity.com
www.travelocity.com

This site is fast and easy to use; gives you lots of flights.

Lowestfare.com
www.lowestfare.com

This site can be persnickety at times because it lists bargain airfares before checking availability. Lowestfare doesn't always live up to its name.

HOTEL DISCOUNTERS

These online room brokers offer a selection of hotel and motel rooms in the U.S. and around the world. They claim that rates are discounted by as much as 50 percent. Availability can be spotty, but check them out.

hoteldiscount!com
www.180096hotel.com

There are thousands of listings for major cities on this site, but sometimes hotel/motel Web sites have better specials, so shop around.

Click-It! Weekends
**www.travelweb.com/TravelWeb/
   clickit.html**

Click here for weekend bargains at upscale hotels (Hilton, Inter-Continental).

HomeExchange.com
www.homeexchange.com

For a $30 annual fee, you can swap houses for a week or two with members anywhere in the world.

CRUISE DISCOUNTERS
CRUISE.COM
www.cruise.com

Here you'll find lots of last-minute deals and early-booking promos. CRUISE.COM guarantees a 10 percent discount off the lowest cruise prices.

The Cruise Web
www.cruiseweb.com

Families shouldn't miss the kids-cruise-free promo on Premier Cruises' Big Red Boat.

Pare down your packing for a less-stressed trip.

TO

FROM

Packed for Pleasure

● Start organizing your clothes the week before you go, laying out everything you think you and your family will need. Then put at least half of the clothes back in the closet. Less is definitely more when it comes to packing. If you're going to a place where you'll have access to a washer-dryer, pack even less.

● Select clothing that gives you the greatest flexibility. Avoid colors that go with only one outfit, for example.

● Don't try to put everyone's clothes in one large suitcase. The suitcase will become unwieldy to handle and messy inside when everyone starts digging through to find their things. Everyone should pack his or her own bag. One exception: One toiletry kit for the family should suffice. Buy small sizes of your regular shampoo, deodorant, and toothpaste. Use disposable razors and pack your favorite scent in solid form.

● Store makeup in an insulated children's lunch box. The insulation keeps the makeup cool and dry and prevents meltdowns.

● In the better-to-be-safe-than-sorry category: Make sure everyone takes a complete change of clothes in a carry-on bag. If your luggage is misplaced, you'll have a set of clothes to change into until you get your bag back.

No guessing dressing! Pack complete outfits—socks, underwear, shirts, shorts—altogether in one see-through bag.

● Another option: "Cross-pack" your suitcases. Put a few of your outfits in his bag, a few of his outfits in yours. That way, if one of your bags gets misplaced or misdirected, you're not entirely without a change of clothes. Do the same for your children.

● Allow for the fact that your kids, maybe even you, will buy a few souvenir T-shirts that can be worn on vacation.

● Choose outfits made of synthetic blends. They're soft and never wrinkle. Look for labels that say "Wash and Wear" or "Drip Dry."

● Bring a lot of accessories—scarves, belts, necklaces, bracelets—to change the look of an outfit. Limit shoes to no more than three pairs: walking shoes or sneakers, casual shoes, and dress shoes—shoes are heavy and bulky.

● Pack several zipper-close plastic bags of various sizes in each suitcase. These can be used to keep dirty clothes away from clean ones, wet clothes away from dry ones, or simply separate out articles of clothing or accessories. Use airtight plastic bags for toiletries that can leak en route, especially when you travel by air.

● Tuck a few dryer fabric-softener sheets into each suitcase as well. Not only will these sheets give your clothes a fresh smell, but they can also be used to de-static outfits.

• Take along a hanger or two (skirt-shirt combo is best) so that you can hang an outfit in a steamy bathroom to remove wrinkles or hang up something you've hand-washed to dry.

• No matter how little you pack, you always come home with more than you started with. Pack a collapsible tote bag in the suitcase to bring home souvenirs and other vacation "finds."

• A small flashlight, penlight, or night-light comes in handy, especially if you're staying in a hotel room. Plug the night-light in so kids can find their way to the bathroom in unfamiliar surroundings. Or keep a flashlight or penlight next to your bed so if you have to get up while others are sleeping, you won't need to turn on a light to find your way.

• As a backup, it's a good idea to take along a travel alarm, even if the hotel provides wake-up calls.

• Never put the following into luggage that you plan to check: tickets, passports, money, traveler's checks, credit cards, medications, glasses, sunglasses, valuable jewelry, address book, and phone numbers you'll need at your destination.

PACK WITH PANACHE

Here are three ways to pack that meet a variety of needs:

Space-saving Fold in shirt sleeves and collars, then roll up the garment. Do the same with pants, shorts, and other garments. Pack large rolls on the suitcase bottom, smaller rolls on top. Squeeze shoes, socks, and other "stuffables" between the rolls. This method packs the most in the suitcase.

Organized by size Lay larger pieces on the bottom with arms and legs hanging over the suitcase sides; lay smaller items on top, then fold the arms and legs of the larger clothes over them. Tuck socks, shoes, and other smaller items around the sides to fill in the gaps. Easy to find what you want; everything stays in place.

Wrinkle-free Place clothes on hangers in dry-cleaning bags; fold and pack directly into the suitcase. Wrap smaller garments in tissue paper and pack them on top. This method takes more space in your suitcase, but it really keeps things wrinkle-free.

Road Rules

Make sure your car is roadworthy and equipped for the possibility of a breakdown. (See *Car Smarts,* pages 139–152.) The American Automobile Association recommends the following:

• No matter how carefully you prepare for your journey, things can go wrong. It's a good idea to keep an emergency kit in your car that contains jumper cables, basic hand tools, flares or reflective warning triangles, a first-aid kit, and a flashlight with fresh batteries.

• Don't leave sharp or heavy objects loose in the car. A sudden stop could turn them into lethal weapons.

• Have the brakes, suspension, and undercarriage of your car checked by a qualified automotive-repair facility.

• Check all fluid levels, including

oil, coolant, windshield washer solution, and battery water. Check windshield wipers, belts, hoses, and tire pressure too.

Miles of Smiles

Long car trips with kids can be, well, challenging. Here's how to make them more enjoyable for everyone:

● Everyone should be buckled up or in appropriate harnesses (age- and weight-appropriate car seats and boosters). Children should sit in the back.

Kids enjoy navigating with their own maps.

● Stop those "when-are-we-going-to-get-there?" questions. Give each child a road map and outline your route. Then let the kids estimate the arrival time, point out landmarks, and calculate gas mileage. They will learn map-reading skills, and you'll get to drive in peace!

● Let the kids help you decide when to take scheduled breaks. Show them the destination for the day on the map, and let them decide how far or how long it should be before a stop.

● If you're driving with children, try to limit the number of hours in the car to four or five a day maximum. Think of the car ride as an integral part of your vacation, not just a means to an end. Stop when you see something of interest, and let the kids out every

couple of hours to run around, stretch their legs, use the rest room, and burn off some excess energy. It's much better to arrive at your destination relaxed and in a positive frame of mind than to be tired, cranky, and disgruntled from a long and uncomfortable car ride.

● You'll need more frequent stops if you're traveling with an infant or pet, so be prepared to stop at least every hour or so and factor that time into the length of your trip.

● Keep a box of surprises — small games, trail mix, crayons, magnetic drawing pads — under your car seat and dole them out to the kids every other hour or so. This encourages good car behavior and keeps boredom at bay.

● Dress kids in comfortable clothing. Take along any favorite stuffed animals.

● Let kids select their own entertainment before you go: books and tapes, CD players with headphones, crossword puzzles, handheld computer games. These can help make those endless highway miles seem less interminable.

● If you have a cassette player in your car, books on tape are a great way to pass the time. Borrow a variety of titles from your local library before you go to keep the cost down.

Tips on Tipping

The following list suggests what are generally considered to be adequate amounts to tip various people for services rendered. Keep in mind that tips are a way of expressing satisfaction. This table is by no means a rule. Use your own judgment when you think amounts should be adjusted up or down.

LOCATION	PERSON	AMOUNT
Airport	Skycaps	$1 or more per bag
	In-flight personnel	None
Cruise ship	Cabin steward	$3 to $3.50 per day per person
	Waiter	$3 per day per person
	Busboy	$1.50 per day per person
	Maitre d'	Your choice; extra for special occasions like birthdays
	Cabin boy, bath steward	5% to 7½% of total fare divided among them, paid at the end of each week
	Bar steward, wine steward	15% tip added to bill automatically
Hotel	Chambermaid	$5 a night minimum, more for long stays (over a week). Consider $7 to $9 a night.
	Room service waiter	15% of bill
	Bellhop	$1 per piece of luggage brought to your room
	Lobby attendant	None for opening door or calling taxi from stand; $1 dollar or more for help with luggage or finding a taxi on the street.
	Desk clerk	None unless special service is given during a long stay, then $5
Limousine	Driver	20% of the bill
Motor coach operator and tour guide(s) (extended tours)	Driver	$1 to $2 per person per day
	Tour guide	$1 to $2 per person per day

● Equip each child with a plastic water bottle so you don't have to deal with "I'm-thirsty" requests every half hour.
● Don't forget some of those tried-and-true car games, such as "I Spy" and "The License Plate Game." (See *Kid Pleasin' Pastimes*, pages 71–80.)

Sane on the Plane

● If you're traveling with an infant, try to get the bulkhead seat, where you will have plenty of room in front of you to put the diaper bag, bottles, and other baby basics.
● Air pressure in the cabin can make little ones' ears hurt. Stock up on hard candies so kids can suck on them as the plane starts to ascend or descend, a method of clearing the ears from pressure.
● Cabin air is always dry. Keep small bottles of water handy for everyone.
● The seats on a plane are confining enough, so dress in comfortable, loose clothing and shoes.

Snap Happy

● Vacations are the stuff great memories—and photo albums—are made of. So don't be an amateur; follow our 12-step program to improve your picture-taking skills:

1. Determine the shape of your subject and hold your camera vertically or horizontally to accommodate it. Don't take a vertical shot of someone lying down, for instance.

2. Study the subject from all sides to decide the best angle from which to take your photo. Consider standing or sitting on a step or a chair or even lying on the floor.

3. Look through the viewfinder and experiment with placing the subject off center for a more striking image.

4. Imagine the picture as it will appear in a frame. Try to close in on the subject to exclude any surrounding distractions that don't belong.

5. Zoom in. Sometimes the subject gets "lost" in a photo when it's taken from a distance. Use a zoom or telephoto lens or physically move closer to the subject.

6. If you're taking a group picture, have everyone interact with each other to reveal distinct personalities. Take a

Frame your photo before you take the shot—you'll get a better picture.

few photos of the group together in case someone is blinking or not captured in a favorable light.

7. Include clues to the size of inanimate objects in your photo. Add an element to the picture that will give a sense of scale. For example, a large tree will look more impressive when photographed with a person standing in front of it.

8. Some things to remember about sunlight or indoor light: The most flattering outdoor light occurs early and late in the day. Direct light, such as the midday sun, will create shadows or wash out the colors of your subject.

With the sun behind you, colors will deepen. Indirect light softens the image.

9. If your developed pictures are usually too dark or washed out, you need to control the contrast. Do so by not aiming the camera toward the sunlight or by using the flash even in outdoor situations.

10. Use a color accent. A red sleigh on a snow-covered hill livens up an otherwise dull background.

11. Reduce red-eye by adding indoor lighting, and do not have your subjects look directly at the camera.

12. Film speed guidelines for 35mm cameras: 100 ASA is best for

Pre-Vacation Plan

Get your vacation off to the best possible start by following this time line.

Select the Dates, Then	A Month Before	Two Weeks Before
● Make arrangements for your children if you intend to travel without them. ● Arrange for your pets to be kenneled if you're leaving them behind. ● If you are traveling abroad, check to see if your passport is valid. If not, get a new one. ● Check to see if you need any vaccinations and make doctor appointments.	● Take a vacation wardrobe inventory. If you're going to a warm-weather spot in the middle of winter, pull out those summer clothes and see what still fits—and if it is suitable. Make a list of what everyone needs and do some shopping each week so the task won't seem overwhelming. ● Check out equipment: camping gear, skiing equipment, cameras, flashlights, binoculars. Make sure everything is in good working order. Replace what's missing.	● Buy traveler's checks and record the numbers. Put the numbers in a spot separate from the checks, and leave a copy of the numbers with someone at home you can call if the checks and your list get lost or stolen. ● Make arrangements to have your plants watered. Stop delivery of the newspaper and mail.

outdoors; 400 ASA is best for inside without flash; and 200 ASA works well in either situation.

Film Fine Points

● To make sure your precious vacation photos come back to you from the developer, on each roll take one shot of a piece of paper with your name, address, and telephone number. That way, if the label gets separated from the film, the photos can still be traced back to you.

● Keep some self-sticking address labels in your camera bag, and affix one to each spent roll of film. This helps prevent store clerks mixing your film with someone else's.

● If you're traveling within the United States, take along some preaddressed and stamped film-developing bags and mail off your film as you travel. You won't have to carry around rolls of spent film—and risk damaging or losing them. And when you get home, your pictures will be waiting for you.

● While on vacation, buy a photo album or two with the destination name on the cover. When you arrive home, put your photos right in the album. There won't be any confusion about where those pictures were taken.

A Week Before	Day Before	Departure Day
● Vacation-proof your home. Store valuables in a safe place, and set timers so lights go on in your absence. If you have an alarm system, let the monitoring company know who will be entering your home in your absence. ● Start packing. (See *Packed for Pleasure*, pages 209–210.) The more time you give yourself to pack, the less chance you'll leave something behind. Check off items on a list as you go. ● Leave an itinerary with a neighbor, friend, or relative, with phone numbers where you can be reached in the event of an emergency.	● Load the car with equipment, gear, and whatever suitcases you won't need the next day. Remember to lock the car before you go to bed. ● Put whatever you plan to take with you the next day—coats, carry-ons— in one designated spot— by the door or on the couch.	● Unplug appliances, empty the dishwasher and wastebaskets, turn down the thermostat, and lock all windows. ● Check your bag and carry-on for tickets, itinerary, traveler's checks. ● Pack drinks, snacks, and wipes.

ACKNOWLEDGMENTS

The best tip for putting together this book? Surround yourself with a crackerjack team of editors, art directors, and designers—they make working on a project like this possible. Thanks to Susan Ungaro, Diane Lamphron, Barbara Winkler, Kathleen Lewandowski, and Angela Ebron for their support, advice, and expertise. Thanks also to Tammy Palazzo for setting the wheels in motion. Special recognition to Laura Cornell for illustrating the book so cleverly. Additional kudos to the entire team at Roundtable Press, without whom there would be no book: Marsha Melnick, Julie Merberg, Susan Meyer, and Carol Spier.

And thanks to all the many people who contributed information to this book. *How to Solve 15 of Life's Little Disasters—Fast,* pages 30–32, was written by Jo Cavallo. *How Long Will It Keep?,* pages 36–37, appears courtesy of the U.S. Department of Agriculture.

Shopping on the Internet: 50 Nifty Web Sites, pages 58–62, was edited by Christina Wood and written by Leslie Crawford (Toys); Anne Kandra (Gift Baskets and Clothes); Michael Lasky (Food, Wine, and Flowers); Glenn McDonald (Movies and Music); Judy Heim (Books and Magazine Subscriptions); and Stan Miastkowski (Electronics). *Banking Online,* page 83, was written by Mike Hogan. *Caring for Your Car,* pages 142–43; the information on what to do in driving emergencies, pages 146–47; and *Car Accident Record,* pages 150–51, appear courtesy of the American Automobile Association, with special thanks to Douglas Love at the AAA Traffic Safety Division. *Stain-Removal Chart,* pages 160–62, appears courtesy of the U.S. Department of Agriculture. James A. Duke, Ph.D. recently retired chief medical herbalist for the U.S. Department of Agriculture, contributed *Healthy Herbs*, page 178. *Travel Bargains Online,* pages 207–208, was written by Donna Heiderstadt.

INDEX